CW00956192

TALES FROM THE
KING'S AFRICAN
RIFLES

★

TALES FROM THE KING'S AFRICAN RIFLES

JOHN NUNNELEY

CASSELL&CO

Cassell & Co
Wellington House, 125 Strand
London WC2R 0BB

A catalogue record for this book is available from the British
Library

ISBN 0-304-35349-3

Designed by Douglas Williamson

Printed and bound in Great Britain by
Redwood Books, Trowbridge, Wilts

Contents

List of Illustrations

Maps

Foreword

by William Boyd

W̲E̲ ̲F̲O̲R̲G̲E̲T̲, all too quickly, how young soldiers are. We forget, or we choose not to remember, that society asks its youngest men – sometimes still boys – to fight its wars on its behalf. This has always been the case since human conflict began, but, in particular, the wars of the twentieth century have been so adulterated by media reinterpretation – fiction, drama, TV, and film – that they have taken on an imaginary life that very often utterly distorts the reality. When you see forty-something actors passing themselves off as twenty-something soldiers – and nobody condemns this as odd, not to say farcical – you realise that the perception of war and warfare (especially from the point of view of those who have no martial experience) can be all too easily suborned in the interests of art – high and low.

Possibly the greatest value, in my opinion, of John Nunneley's fine and enthralling memoir of his experience of the Second World War is that it reminds us, unobtrusively and with great subtlety, of his extreme youth at the time. He was 18 when he was commissioned as a second lieutenant into the Somerset Light Infantry in 1941. He was 21 years old, and a captain, when he was fighting for his life in the steaming jungle battles of the Kabaw Valley in Burma in 1944. Somehow – it is no easy task – the author manages to reinhabit his younger self perfectly, and though the book is full of the benefits and reflective wisdom of hindsight, it is also vivid with the freshness and guilelessness and innocence of a 20-year-old going to war. We see events, we understand judgements, we experience shock and horror, as if we are peering through the eyes and sensibility of a very young man.

There is absolutely nothing affected in this, nothing *faux-naif* at all. Its achievement, I would surmise, arises out of a combination of almost total recall, an absolute candour and a complete avoidance of irony or wisdom-after-the-event. Our younger selves are often the source of humour, or dismay, or deep embarrassment to us, but that is how we were and our experiences and emotions had a validity then – and a potent impact – that is sometimes lacking in the maturer adult we become. John Nunneley has replicated this vivacity and immediacy with tremendous skill and it allows the book to deliver a charge of empathy – of real fellow-feeling – that is extremely rare.

Consequently we follow him on his journey through 1940–5 with unusual insight and sympathy: from the surreal strangeness of being a white officer in an African regiment, guarding Italian prisoners of war (men and women) in Abyssinia and Somaliland, to the veritable hell of Burma in 1944. John Nunneley's detailed and unsparing accounts of the brutal skirmishes and firefights in the Kabaw Valley, as the British and Empire forces pursued the retreating Japanese to the Chindwin, reek with authenticity as well as all the chaos and terror, the sheer blind luck and cruel tragedy of battle. This is writing that is palpably, heart-stoppingly effective and I believe that these episodes – and the uniquely special witness that John Nunneley bears – make *Tales from the King's African Rifles* a work of real and lasting importance to the literature of war.

Introduction

IN A SINGLE PARAGRAPH Africa's potent spell is cast upon the reader of Moyse-Bartlett's history of the King's African Rifles: 'No regiment has ever been more intimately connected with the territories through which it marched and fought, or with the peoples from whom it was recruited. Among the lakes and uplands of Central Africa, the swamps and rivers of Uganda, the mountains and deserts of the Abyssinian border, and the waterless bush of Somaliland, the operations of the King's African Rifles have played a major part in the development of British Africa.'

The origins of the KAR lie in the heart of the five Great Powers' nineteenth-century 'Scramble for Africa', when the Dark Continent was carved up into unequal portions and shared out among them according to their political, military, and economic muscle. The avowed aim of each country was to end slavery and bring Christianity, civilisation, and commerce to a hundred million backward people considered to be standing in desperate need of these blessings. Before 1880 much of the continent of Africa remained to be explored by Europeans. Less than thirty years later, only Liberia and Abyssinia remained unconquered by them. The Central and East Africa 'grab' began in 1884, when Karl Peters, a German explorer, made treaties with a number of chiefs. The following year saw the founding of the German East Africa Company which soon afterwards received a Charter of Protection from the Kaiser. Germany was following on the heels of a British initiative: Harry Johnston, also an explorer, had already made treaties in East Africa's Moshi and Taveta areas. Britain, France, and Germany agreed to abide by the recommendations of an international commission which they set up to define their 'spheres of influence' and

Johnston's treaties were taken over by the British East Africa Association formed for the purpose. In 1888 the association was granted a royal charter and became the Imperial British East Africa Company charged with responsibility to administer an enormous territory along the lines of a Crown Colony.

A dispute between the German and British companies concerning territorial boundaries was settled by the Anglo-German Agreement of 1890 so that Britain's southern boundary now ran inland from the Umba River to Lake Jipe, skirting Kilimanjaro so that the mountain was included in the German sphere, to continue westward across Lake Victoria along the line of 1 degree south latitude to the boundary of the Congo Free State. Under this agreement Britain's sphere now included a vast area extending to the western watershed of the Nile. It was not long before the need became apparent for some form of military or police force to assist the British company's administration of the territories, and to prevent inter-tribal conflicts, protect trading operations, and suppress the Arabs' slave trade. Small bands of tribesmen were therefore recruited, armed, and led by the company's British agents until necessity caused each territory to form its own regiment, strengthened by Sudanese who had formerly served in the Khedive of Egypt's army, Indian contingents, and local levies. The Mahdi's rebellion had driven these Sudanese south out of the Sudan and now, serving under Emin Pasha, they were the basis of the Uganda Rifles. It was they whose subsequent influence introduced 'effendis' into the King's African Rifles.

In Nyasaland the Arabs' hostility to interference with their slaving trade, whose caravans were well supplied with arms, was understandable. The slaver, Mlozi, a coastal Arab, and others in the trade, had long since established routes across the southern end of Lake Nyasa and now looked to develop the northern end by building stockades at Karonga, on the northwest shore of the lake, as another inland power base. For its part, the African Lakes Company had built a trading station at Karonga as this was the point of departure of the Stevenson Road and a first step in the route from the Cape to Cairo. The company felt threatened by Mlozi's attempt to extend Arab influence over the inland areas and reacted strongly so that in 1888 what became known as the Slavers' War began and continued until 1896, the year when the Central Africa Rifles was brought into being.

Uganda in 1890 was on the brink of civil war as the Muslims and their Arab allies prepared an attack on Buganda from Bunyoro. The Christians had become divided so that the Anglican chiefs supported the treaty with the British company, while the Catholic chiefs were suspicious and covertly hostile. It was to ease this situation that the British Government exerted pressure and Captain Lugard, who had taken service with the Imperial British East Africa Company, arrived in Buganda to persuade King Mwanga to sign a treaty with the company. Lugard realised that if he was to succeed in his task of composing the differences between the hostile factions and 'to instruct Mwanga in the art of impartial kingship', he needed the means of upholding his own authority and maintaining the company's prestige. He therefore strengthened his tiny force of 50 Sudanese and Somalis and a Maxim machine-gun with another 75 Sudanese, 100 Swahili, and a second Maxim gun. It was from this nucleus that the Uganda Rifles was formed.

The East Africa Rifles developed from the Imperial British East Africa Company's recognition that it needed troops or armed police to provide a force at its back. This need became more urgent when the balance of the company's interests in the territory's economic development was changing from the coast to the highlands, and the administrative and commercial centre was moved from Dar es Salaam to a small inland settlement which would become the city of Nairobi. The Foreign Office took over responsibility from the company when the territories were brought together as the East Africa Protectorates and it was decided that the three regiments should be amalgamated as different battalions within a single regiment. On 1 January 1902 the King's African Rifles came into being. The 1st and 2nd Battalions emerged from the Central Africa

Rifles; the 3rd Battalion, from the East Africa Rifles, included a camel company; the 4th and 5th Battalions were created from the Uganda Rifles; and the 6th (Somaliland) Battalion would be formed somewhat later of three infantry companies, the camel corps, militia, and mounted infantry of the local forces in Somaliland. On the disbandment of the 6th Battalion it was re-formed of askaris who had served in German East Africa's Schutztruppe which had fought against Britain in the East Africa Campaign of 1914–18. The new regiment was designated 'Rifles' because all the original regiments had at some time been so called, but the men drilled as infantry, most of the officers and all the Indian troops who had served in them also being infantry. The regiment's officers were seconded from the Regular Army for five-year periods and were supplemented, if need be, by officers of the Militia, Imperial Yeomanry, and Reserve of Officers.

Following four successive Expeditions against the Mad Mullah in Somaliland, the campaign in German East Africa in the First World War of 1914–18 saw the regiment expanded to twenty-two battalions comprising almost 30,000 Africans led by 1,300 officers and 1,900 British non-commissioned officers. In 1915 Lieutenant-Colonel S.H. Shepherd wrote: 'The KAR . . . hardly ever lose a rifle . . . The conclusion is the same that every thinking soldier in the force has arrived at after a year in British East Africa, namely that only the best and most highly trained troops, British or Indian, are or can hope to be a match for the trained Africans of a fighting tribe in the bush.' This unstinting praise was well-deserved and hard-won: by the end of the war a total of 7,700 Africans and 430 Europeans had been listed as 'killed, wounded, or died of disease'.

A generation later the monsoon campaign of 1944 against the Japanese in the Burma jungle represented the most strenuous test to be faced by the regiment since the First World War. Even so, as Moyse-Bartlett observes: 'Burma could not compare, either in length of operations, distance covered, hardship involved, or casualties sustained, with the years 1917–18, which still remain the highlight of the Regiment's history. In

4

many aspects of jungle warfare African troops proved out-standing. Their great physical strength enabled them to make long marches across rough country, carrying mortars, ammunition and other heavy loads. Their cheerfulness under the worst climatic conditions never failed. Their eyesight, especially at night, and their sense of hearing, was markedly better than those of Europeans. African platoon commanders and NCOs did first-rate patrol work, a duty that took heavy toll of Europeans, so much so that some senior officers actually preferred to entrust reconnaissance, as apart from fighting, patrols to the leadership of Africans.

'The "defence-and-delay" tactics of the Japanese in Burma as they retreated down the disease-ridden Kabaw Valley, "The Valley of Death", varied little. Mutually supporting bunker positions were usually constructed covering the road, often on small knolls occupied only by a platoon in slit trenches manning machine guns. These positions would be "bumped" by forward patrols who withdrew when the Japanese opened fire. Air strikes which blasted away the camouflage, trees, and undergrowth would then "uncover" the enemy positions, following which the infantry would go in under cover of artillery. Sometimes the position would be found evacuated, but more often it was discovered that the Japanese had descended to the safety of a nearby chaung during the airstrike and had now returned unharmed to await the attack. If the enemy were still manning the position the attack had to be completed by the platoon commander and his African troops, with their bayonets, pangas, and grenades. The outcome of the fighting depended largely upon the initiative of the junior leader, ideally reinforced by a strong bond of trust grown between him and his askaris during their service together.'

Against the Germans in the First World War, in the Abyssinian Campaign of 1940-1 against the Italians, in Madagascar in 1942-3 against the forces of Vichy France, and in the Burma Campaign advancing against 'the best jungle fighters in the world', the qualities of the KAR askaris were tested and proved again and again in reconnaissance and fighting patrol, in close-quarter skirmish, and set-piece battle. In the regiment's short life – little more than fifty years from its creation as a peace-keeping instrument of Empire to the independence of the countries it had been raised to serve – its battalions from Kenya, Uganda, Tanganyika, and Nyasaland had maintained the highest traditions of the British Army at the same time as they nurtured a fine pride in their own.

Fate's Decree

THERE RUNS THROUGHOUT these tales a thread, sometimes there for all to see, at other times concealed. It is the story of a young African tribesman, a Luo from the Kenya shores of Lake Victoria. His name was Kitinya until the Catholic missionaries converted him from paganism and gave him a saint's name so that he became known thereafter as Tomasi Kitinya, son of Liech. At the time of our first meeting I guessed his age to be 16 but he might have been younger. To tell Tomasi's story as it deserves to be told I have gone back to the very beginning, to the events that threw our lives together and carried us halfway across the world. Because these are tales of wartime I have given the names of armies and divisions and brigades, of regiments and battalions, of companies and, sometimes, even platoons so that Tomasi may take his honourable and singular place in the history of the Second World War.

For me, the beginning was in Cornwall. As a very young second lieutenant newly-commissioned into the Somerset Light Infantry (Prince Albert's) I was posted to the 9th Battalion stationed at Pen-y-Gillam Camp on the outskirts of Launceston. Straight from 166 Officer Cadet Training Unit in the Isle of Man I reported for duty on 14 September 1941, and found myself second-in-command of a platoon of thirty men. This was not a situation which appealed to me; to all intents and purposes I and a number of other subalterns were surplus to the battalion's requirements. There was a good reason for this surplus. The officer-producing units were working at full stretch to meet the Army's huge expansion needs so that by the middle of 1941 there were more platoon commanders than there were platoons for them to lead. Moreover, it has always been the case that proportionately the casualty rate amongst platoon commanders is so high that a full reservoir of replacements must be maintained. These strategic considerations cut no ice with me and I resolved to obtain a posting where I would see action and derring-do against the enemy.

Insignificant events may have important consequences. If I had not found myself a 'second fiddle' platoon commander I might have remained in the narrow groove of British regimental soldiering for the duration of the war and missed years of adventure and drama in seven countries and two continents. An escape route seemed to be open to me. Several times each week notices would appear on a board outside the adjutant's office calling for volunteers for all manner of postings at home and abroad. These invitations held a special attraction to junior officers in my predicament and all that appeared to be necessary was to apply, and keep on applying, for anything and everything until one struck lucky. My principal goal was the Middle East, where there was enough fighting to satisfy the most warlike of young men, and it was only a few weeks before my plan worked although not in the way I wanted. After several disappointments I was accepted for 'special service in the Far East' and ordered to report to a holding unit in Leeds after seven days' embarkation leave. Any regrets I had in failing to get to the Middle East were countered by what promised to be a splendid opportunity to travel across the world to exotic lands at no expense to myself.

The thirty junior infantry officers who made up Draft RAKYK enjoyed a life of luxury aboard His Majesty's Transport *Scythia*, a 19,000-ton Cunarder built for the prestigious North Atlantic run. The crew, retained in wartime, included chefs of impressive skill and stewards whose discreet efficiency had been a byword among peacetime first-class passengers. Breakfast, lunch, and dinner menus were elegantly printed on stiff, gilt-edged card and offered dazzling choice. Caviare was served several times each week, and the wine list was judged, by those who knew much more about it than I, to be superb. Napery, cutlery, glass, and china complemented perfectly-cooked meals, and the cocktail bar offered gin and whisky at threepence a large measure. There was much to be said in favour of cruising First Class to war. If fault had to be found it was in the accommodation. Life would have been even more agreeable if each of us had had a cabin to himself rather than four having to share. On the whole, though, we rubbed along well enough together except towards the end of the six-week voyage when tempers grew short and occasionally were lost altogether for the most trivial reasons. In an unseemly brawl I broke a middle finger beyond repair in inflicting damage on Second Lieutenant Gibbs of the Lancashire Fusiliers. After the voyage he and I did not meet for almost three years, when we found ourselves once again sharing accommodation. This time it was at a tented casualty clearing station at Khampat airstrip hacked out of the Burma jungle, he having taken a burst of Japanese machine-gun fire in the arm, and me with leg wounds. Our stretchers, we agreed, were much less comfortable than *Scythia*'s bunks.

The Japanese attack on Pearl Harbour on 7 December 1941 took place while the convoy was at sea en route for the Cape of Good Hope and beyond to the Far East. Within days Malaya and South-East Asia as a whole were threatened with invasion and the decision was taken to halt the flow of reinforcements other than those convoys which were even now approaching Singapore, the 'Impregnable Fortress'. It was rumoured that the scores of thousands of troops in our convoy, the biggest ever to have left Britain at that time, were to be switched to the Middle East, East Africa, and India. Of these three the Middle East remained my goal.

There was endless excitement as the convoy ploughed through the Atlantic at the speed of the slowest ship. Protecting us, the battleship *Ramillies* was supported by a dozen or so destroyers which raced through heavy seas urging captains to keep station. Scarcely a day or night passed without the distant flash and reverberating thunder of guns and depth charges fuelling rumours of torpedoings far out on the flanks and U-boats sunk, but we hoped that the troop transports forming the inner lines of the convoy might be relatively safe. Our route had taken us far north across the Atlantic in an attempt to avoid enemy submarines hunting in the Western Approaches before we changed course to head for Freetown in Sierra Leone for fuel and water. As the weather warmed up and winter clothing was exchanged for tropical gear, the voyage became even more of a holiday cruise. Regular and frequent 'Boat Stations' exercises were carried out and the mess decks inspected daily in the maintenance of general shipboard discipline, but for the officers of Draft RAKYK travelling without troops under command, responsibilities were light.

I seemed always to be first in the cabin to wake in the morning. No doubt stretching and yawning as I looked out of the porthole on the morning of 22 December I had a surprise: there was not another ship to be seen. That the ocean around us was completely empty of vessels was confirmed when I sprinted up on deck. To make matters worse, *Scythia* was barely moving, managing perhaps five knots at best as engine-room staff strove to make repairs. In minutes near panic broke out among many of the troops as word went round and they surged on deck to see for themselves that not a single destroyer had been left to protect us from Dakar-based U-boats. I was glad that ours was an all-male ship. It is all very well to recall the story of the sinking of the *Birkenhead*, when the troops stood fast on deck as the ship went down and the women and children took to the lifeboats, but in enemy-infested waters one tends to view events in a different light. The realisation that a torpedo might strike home at any moment was sobering even for young men who believed themselves to be immortal. In our case the potential for outright panic was heightened because most of those on board were Royal Air Force tradesmen, civilians in uniform, so to speak, whose only experience of military discipline was a few weeks' parade-ground drill as recruits before being posted overseas.

★ ★ ★

Young and lacking in experience as I was, I had already witnessed panic in the ranks. That was at Hawkinge and Lympne advanced airfields in the South-East's 'Hell Fire Corner' of

Kent, when yellow-nosed Messerschmitt Bf109E fighters of the Luftwaffe's crack Jagdgeschwader 26, famed as the 'Abbeville Kids', bombed and strafed us during the Battle of Britain and in the months that followed. I was then a lance-corporal in The Buffs, the Royal East Kent Regiment, first formed in 1572 and the third oldest regiment of foot in the British Army. I commanded a Lewis machine-gun section and was having the time of my life firing 98-round drums of ball, tracer, incendiary and armour-piercing ammunition at the enemy diving to the attack, each with two 7.9mm machine guns and three 20mm cannon flashing from the nose and leading edge of their wings before they dropped their bombs and raced for home across the Channel.

The first of my nine or more wartime lives was used up one calm, cloudless Sunday evening early in May 1941 when twelve Me109s made a leisurely, high half-circuit of Lympne airfield before changing formation from line astern to line abreast and beginning their dive. Perhaps under the impression that these were friendly fighters it was only then that the anti-aircraft guns began to bark. One enemy pilot had targeted my Lewis-gun post and opened fire with his machine guns and cannon. I replied with a full drum and a head-on duel was fought man-to-man between us before the fighter swept directly overhead, almost at ground level, and zoomed away. That he had missed us by a whisker was revealed when thin wisps of smoke from his cannonshells rose from the ground just three yards from the gun-pit. I was confident that he could not have escaped unscathed and later learned that several of the Messerschmitts had crashed after leaving us and before reaching Manston airfield, their second target of the raid. I hoped that one of them was 'mine'.

It was at Hawkinge, at the height of a devastating raid, that we lost a comrade when Private Nash was mown down in a burst of Me109 cannon fire. I was detailed a member of the Firing Party, which the Regimental Sergeant-Major rehearsed again and again in the essentials of a military funeral with full honours: the slow march with a momentary pause mid-stride and boot-toe pointed; the slow reversing of arms from the 'Present' and back again; three volleys, perfectly synchronised, fired over the grave; the 'Port Arms' for inspection; and the Bugler sounding the 'Last Post' without a false note. We buried Nash in the airfield cemetery. He was our first war casualty and his Army service totalled just three months.

Not everybody felt as exhilarated as I did during the raids; perhaps I lacked the imagination that others may have had in abundance. Many RAF ground crew and a few Buffs lost their heads in the racket as bombs came screaming down to explode in crimson flame, smoke, and thunder while buildings burst asunder, and our fighter aircraft and ground defences fought back. Some men grabbed rifles and fired at shot-down airmen dangling helplessly on their parachutes, convinced that they were in the front line of an airborne invasion, that Hitler's 'Operation Sea Lion' had been launched against Britain. Twice I had to wrest rifles away to prevent indiscriminate attempted murder. Fortunately for the intended victims, whether British or German nobody could tell, their attackers were so terrified they could barely hold a rifle, let alone aim with any degree of accuracy even at a slowly-descending target. So much for discipline and training, I thought, and stored the experience away as a lesson to be remembered. Leaving aside such inevitable tragedies of war as the casualties, for me this was a ripping *Boy's Own Paper* yarn come to life with myself as hero, and when my posting came through for officer-training I had my regrets at leaving the battlefield.

★   ★   ★

After the initial panic the men on board *Scythia* settled down pretty well although not surprisingly great numbers insisted on sleeping on deck rather than deep down in the mess-decks. I could understand their point of view but preferred the comfort of my cabin. With 2,000 troops on board *Scythia* would be rich pickings for the U-boat commander who found us wallowing along at little more than a light infantryman's brisk pace. Not only could he have come easily within torpedo range, with only our single, stern-mounted gun to oppose him, he might even with little risk to himself sink us with gunfire to conserve his heavy ordnance. A few of us had made up 'survival haversacks' containing the bare essentials which might give us a chance of enduring days in the ship's boats or on Carley floats, but the vast majority of men were clearly unprepared both mentally and practically for what might so easily happen. The order would be 'every man for himself' if the ship went down and I was determined to be a survivor, come what may. The three days it took to reach Freetown seemed much, much longer. As *Scythia* at last steamed slowly into harbour ships' sirens blared in welcome, thousands of men lining the decks cheered us to our mooring and a signal from *Ramillies* congratulated us on our safe arrival made against the odds. It was Christmas Day, most appropriate for prayers of thanksgiving for our deliverance from the perils of wartime seas.

★ ★ ★

The war in the Far East got off to a bad start for the Allies as Japan overran one country after another in a seemingly unstoppable orgy of blitzkrieg warfare. Held back at Durban until London decided that Draft RAKYK was to be switched to East Africa we waited for three weeks at the Imperial Forces Transit Camp at Clairwood, a few miles outside the city. It was not until 31 January 1942 that we embarked on the Holland-America Line flagship *Nieuw Amsterdam* and sailed for Mombasa. The threat now was from Japanese, Italian, and German submarines prowling the Mozambique Channel and the western Indian Ocean and enjoying a run of success in sinking Allied ships. A high-speed dash saw us through with little more than a scare or two and on 4 February the ship dropped anchor in Mombasa's great natural harbour. Two days later our troop-train steamed into Nairobi.

★ ★ ★

In the Horn of Africa the Italian commander-in-chief, the Duke of Aosta, had led an army of 350,000 deployed in Eritrea, Abyssinia, and Italian Somaliland supported by a navy which seemed likely to command both the Mediterranean and the Red Sea. The duke had been reinforced with a strong air force,

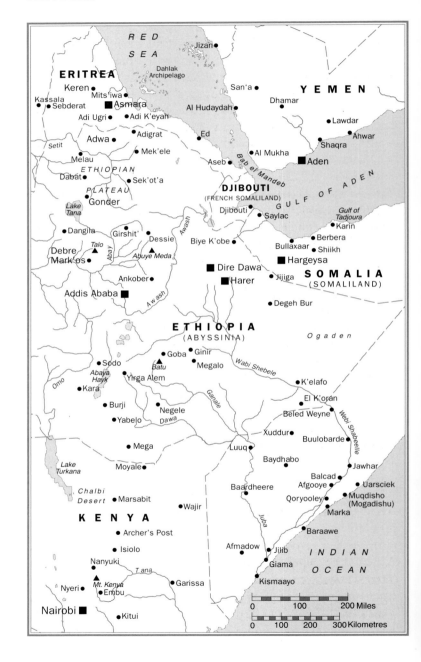

plus artillery and the Bersaglieri, Savoy Grenadiers, and Alpini, three elite regiments whose training fitted them perfectly for Abyssinia's mountain terrain. It was Mussolini's ambition to use his African armies to throw out the British and to expand the Italian Empire on a scale to rival that of his Axis partner, Germany. The first step of the strategy was to tighten his control of the southern entrance to the Red Sea and on 5 August, 1940 the invasion of British Somaliland was launched. The garrison of 1,500 King's African Rifles and British troops fought bravely against overwhelming odds in that brief and little-known campaign, giving the Italians such a bloody nose that our troops were able to withdraw unhindered and in good order. Their evacuation from Berbera by sea allowed Mussolini to proclaim 'a magnificent victory' which, he promised, would now be followed by a total blockade of all British possessions in Africa and the Mediterranean.

Five months later, General Wavell, the commander-in-chief, ordered Lieutenant-General Sir William Platt in the Sudan to stir up rebellion in Abyssinia and to recapture Kassala in the spring of 1941 with two Indian divisions. His strategy called for a gigantic pincer movement, its two claws 1,200 miles apart at the outset. Down in Kenya the commander of the British forces was directed to threaten the Italians at Moyale on Kenya's northern border and to advance on Kismayu, on the Juba River, once the rains were over. For this purpose Lieutenant-General Alan Cunningham was allotted 11 (African) Division comprising King's African Rifles battalions from Kenya, Tanganyika, Uganda, Nyasaland and the Northern Rhodesia Regiment; 1 (South African) Division; and, from West Africa, 12 (African) Division together with 23 (Nigerian) Brigade and 24 (Gold Coast) Brigade.

Even before the Indian divisions could reach Kassala the Italians evacuated it and took refuge in the great mountain fortress of Keren, where the road passes through a deep, precipitous ravine. Supported by as many as 144 guns the 30,000 infantry of the Italian Army fought hard and well, launching one unsuccessful counter-attack after another until their eighth was also repulsed with heavy losses and Keren fell. The siege was costly to both sides: the British forces suffered 4,000 casualties killed, wounded, and missing; and the Italians 3,000 killed. The victory at Keren brought effective resistance in Eritrea to an end. On 1 April the city of Asmara fell with thousands of prisoners taken and the vitally-important port of Massawa surrendered two days later.

To the south Cunningham's divisions beat the Italians on the Juba River in February, then pressed on nearly three hundred miles with motorised infantry to capture Mogadishu three weeks later. Astonished at the weak resistance offered by the Italians Cunningham set out for Jijiga, almost eight hundred miles away, en route to retake the ancient 'Forbidden City' of Harar. First Jijiga fell, then Berbera surrendered to a small seaborne force sent across the Gulf from Aden, followed by the capitulation of Harar on 25 March. In thirty days the British advance had covered more than one thousand miles with an average of 35 miles a day, a remarkable feat of arms and logistics over atrocious terrain.

As Wavell's pincer claws closed Addis Ababa was abandoned early in April, then Dessie, a hundred miles to the north, fell to Cunningham as the Duke of Aosta's Eritrean Army retired south along the Asmara–Addis Ababa road to stand at Amba Alagi, a natural stronghold. On 20 January 1941 Emperor Haile Selassie, the Lion of Judah, had re-entered his country (which he had fled in 1936) at a little place called Um Idla, on the plain of the Blue Nile 30 miles inside the Abyssinian border. He returned, in Churchill's words, as 'the first of the lawful sovereigns to be driven from his throne by the Fascist-Nazi criminals'. On his entry into Addis Ababa on 5 May the King's African Rifles found the Emperor's Guard of Honour.

Although Aosta had elected to fight on ground of his own choosing, most desirable in war, the campaign was virtually over by the middle of May, for the Italians' water supply had failed and Aosta had no option but to surrender unconditionally. Wavell acknowledged the Italians' chivalry – there was no bombing of the civilian population, no deportations, wanton destruction, rape, murder, or plundering, unlike their behaviour in the 1935 invasion of Abyssinia to which they added the use of mustard gas on a defenceless people – and granted the duke the honours of war. The Italian troops cleared the battlefield of mines, handed over guns, equipment, and stores intact and were allowed to march out carrying their personal weapons. General Nasi held out in Gondar Province for a further six months of hard fighting in which a large force of KAR, including two newly-raised brigades, suffered the heaviest casualties of the entire Abyssinian Campaign. By November effective resistance in Gondar Province came to an end, hastened by guerilla activity in Western Abyssinia.

The reconquest of the Horn of Africa cleared lines of communication up the Red Sea. The brief war had cost Mussolini his dreams of Empire at the expense of the lives of thousands of his soldiers, and the survivors of his African Army were now prisoners of war. The 34,000 Italian colonist population was interned while the International Red Cross negotiated repatriation.

★   ★   ★

It was bad enough that my Far East posting had come to a full stop far short of destination; now I had arrived in Africa too late to take part in the Abyssinian campaign. This was a real setback. However, there was still the slight chance of a transfer to the Middle East and I at once lay siege to the Military Secretary, Lieutenant-Colonel Lord Francis Scott, just as my hero, Nelson, had persistently presented himself to Their Lordships of the Admiralty as deserving of a command. Reluctantly acknowledging to myself that second lieutenants carry little weight in the Army's corridors of power I nevertheless lived in hope at the oddly-named Base Details Camp on the outskirts of Nairobi while my fate was being decided. In peacetime Base Details had been the headquarters of the Kenya Regiment. The colonial-style buildings were principally of timber construction and were raised on brick piers as protection against the white ants that munch their relentless way through wood. In addition to numerous offices, brick-built armouries and stores there was the Officers' Mess, the largest and most imposing building of all, with a verandah which extended across the entire frontage and overlooked the parade ground. At this time the camp was the hub of East Africa Command's massive expansion accelerated by the demands of the Abyssinian campaign and by plans being formulated to send a division to fight the Japanese in South-East Asia. Drafts of officers, non-commissioned officers, and men of all arms and services flooded in from Britain and the Rhodesias to train and lead the hundreds of thousands of African tribesmen who had been encouraged or persuaded, even ordered, by their chiefs to volunteer to fight for 'Kingi Georgie'.

I wondered what lay in store for me.

★ ★ ★

For Tomasi life began in earnest when he found his first job near his village of Agoro. Until then his had been a typical Luo childhood: a few carefree years larking in the shallows of Lake Victoria with his friends; early responsibility as his father's herd-boy and helping his mother to cultivate their shamba; and attendance at the White Fathers' mission school where he learned to say his prayers and read and write. When Tomasi was 13 the missionaries gave him a 'chit' testifying to his good character and zeal, confident that this would prove his passport to gaining employment with the Wazungu, the White People. Sure enough, very soon he fell on his feet: he was taken on as 'kitchen mtoto' by a European settler whose farm lay close to Agoro.

The life of a kitchen 'toto is that of a 'gofer' he is a domestic dogsbody at the beck and call of the mpishi, the cook. No matter how hard, how demanding, the work he must do it without complaint for the 'toto who displeases the mpishi risks his job. A kindly mpishi is a pleasure to work for, a man who teaches as much as he commands, and Tomasi was fortunate that this was the nature of his first master. Quickly, because he was bright and eager and keen-eyed, and listened attentively to his memsahib as she spoke 'kitchen-Swahili' and her own English language, Tomasi learned many of the ways of the Wazungu. I guess he was a model 'toto, for he stayed with the settler's family for three years before the urge to move on became too strong to resist. He explained to his father and mother his wish to find a different way of life, seeking also the advice of the White Father and the mpishi and, last of all, the memsahib. He had shown the Wazungu that he was trustworthy, reliable, and anxious to learn, and felt ready to launch himself on the world. All were agreed: armed with his kipande he should make his way to distant Nairobi to look for work in a European household.

The kipande was worth its weight in gold to the job-seeker. Without this booklet, in which successive employers wrote references and assessments of the bearer's character, honesty, and willingness, it was hard even to be granted an interview. 'No kipande, no job' was the general rule. Tomasi had no problem in that respect: the memsahib wrote well of his work, the White Father praised his character and spiritual qualities. Full of hope and confidence he made his farewells and hitch-hiked to Nairobi with just a few shillings in savings in his pocket.

War brings opportunities and very shortly after his arrival in the huge, teeming city some kindly soul advised Tomasi to try for employment with the Army; there were, he learned, thousands of Wazungu at the great camp outside the city looking for servants and with his kipande he stood as good a chance as anybody of being taken on by one of them. Already I had begun to realise the need for a personal servant, a man to wash my clothes, polish boots and brass, fetch and carry, make and tend fires. When I joined a battalion as a platoon commander I would have an orderly for military tasks, such as a runner, but except in war zones an orderly did not perform domestic duties for his officer. A personal servant was enrolled into the Army; he was not enlisted as a private soldier. He was a civilian, the direct employee of the officer who paid his wages of around thirty shillings a month and took full responsibility for him. For its part, the Army provided food and accommodation and, of course, transport so that he could accompany his master at all times. He could be dismissed at a moment's notice – there was no 'contract' other than a handshake – and he could resign without notice. The Army undertook to return him to his native country if he were serving outside its borders. It was a simple arrangement for all three parties involved and one that worked well.

I was not finding it easy to organise my evening bath. Hot water had to be scrounged and carried by the canvas bucket-load to the Lines to fill my collapsible bath erected outside the tent I shared with another new arrival. Once used, the water must be emptied back into the bucket and carried to a distant drain in compliance with strictly-enforced tropical hygiene rules. There was also the matter of early-morning shaving water and a mug of tea to worry about. And who was to dhobi and starch my cotton-drill uniforms and press them with a charcoal iron? My posting would come through any day now and I must have a servant to accompany me. Squatting cross-legged in the bath one evening, in that magical hour in Africa when the sun goes down, and using an old canned-fruit tin as makeshift shower, I noticed a lanky, very black youth walking along the Lines towards me, a shy smile on his face. His shirt and shorts were spotlessly clean and his cheerful, open face was heavily cicatriced with tribal markings. The sundown hour was the time of day that offered those in the labour market the best chance of finding a potential employer 'at home', so to speak. Without quite knowing why, I had already waved away a number who had approached me that evening, and on previous evenings, vaguely feeling that their faces did not fit, but something told me I should give this boy a hearing.

Neither of us spoke the other's language but this was no problem. Having read his kipande and trusting to instinct I engaged Tomasi Kitinya, son of Liech, as my personal servant. The date: 8 February 1942.

By fate's decree Tomasi's life and mine had been brought together.

In Breach of Convention

T HE MORE I thought about that last-minute switch of Draft RAKYK to East Africa the more I counted myself lucky to have escaped the fate of the 150,000 British, Australian, and Indian troops who were now prisoners of war following the ignominious surrender of Singapore on 15 February 1942. The convoy to the Far East which had sailed from Britain a month ahead of ours included an entire Army division which arrived on 29 January and whose 20,000 men had never fired a shot before being herded off with the troops already there to suffer years of privation and indiscriminate brutality by their Japanese and Korean guards. Bitterness, resentment, and frustration – even a deep sense of shame that they had been prevented from doing their duty in fighting the Japanese – were to stay with many of the survivors for the rest of their lives. As for me, here I was, suddenly set down in Africa as though by a giant hand and evidently destined to command black soldiers called 'askaris'.

It was a fortunate coincidence that I already had a vicarious familiarity with Britain's African Empire. Years before the outbreak of war I had read with bug-eyed fascination books on the first and second Zulu Wars of 1879 and 1883, wishing I had been born early enough to distinguish myself in them; the rights and wrongs of Britain's colonial policy was too deep a subject for a 12-year-old and I avoided such complex issues in favour of tales of gallantry against King Cetewayo's massed impis. The South Wales Borderers' stand at Rorke's Drift, when 160 brave men fought off wave after wave of Zulu assaults; the disaster at Isandhlwana – 66 officers and 731 rank and file speared and hacked and disembowelled by between 12,000 and 20,000 Zulu warriors – attributed to a commander who unaccountably led his force forward from a strong defensive position to open country; and the charge of the 17th Lancers at the Battle of Ulundi fired up my imagination. In all these engagements with the savage enemy I was there, more often than not saving the Colours.

Time and again I put myself in Lieutenant Carey's position as I pondered the circumstances and implications of the death in action of the young Prince Imperial, only son of Emperor Napoleon III and Empress Eugenie of France. The burning question was: in his situation, would I have acted as Lieutenant Carey had? Whereas Victorian and Edwardian writers of Empire adventure stories for boys invariably portrayed bravery and cowardice and duty in stark, black-and-white terms there must in real life be a multitude of grey areas, I reasoned, of which the prince's tragic death was surely an example? Consider the facts. The prince, at his repeated request and against his adoring mother's better judgement – a woman's intuition perhaps – was to be allowed to join the commander-in-chief's staff as a 'spectator' of the Zulu War, with no military rank. Should he choose to wear a uniform no objections would be raised. In his opinion he was well-prepared for campaigning: ardent, young, physically fit, a bold horseman, and a fine swordsman taught by the best instructors in France and England. All he craved was a chance to win glory against Cetewayo's warriors.

In March 1879 the prince arrived in Cape Town and reported for attachment. Understandably the general, with a war to win, would have preferred to be spared responsibility for a young prince of the blood royal of France but bowed loyally to the wishes of his sovereign, Queen Victoria, a close friend of the widowed empress living near to her in England. In the weeks following his arrival the prince, impatient to see action, pressed to be allowed out on patrol and each time the C.-in-C. denied him his opportunity. On 1 June Lieutenant Carey of the Royal Engineers, attached to Army headquarters, was ordered to make sketches of a strategically-important area. A corporal and five men of 3 Troop, Natal Horse would act as escort and protection against unlikely but possible attack, and a 'friendly' Zulu would serve as guide. The Prince Imperial would accompany the patrol. Within this seemingly-simple order was sown in Carey's mind the seed of disaster. Was he, a Regular officer, the leader of the patrol – or was the prince leader as being senior to him by virtue of his noble birth although junior to him in military terms? With this unspoken question of fundamental importance unresolved the patrol set out.

Some hours later and the sketches made, the patrol halted for a short rest at a small group of empty grass-thatched huts on the edge of tall, growing maize. Sentries were not posted but, apprehensive that they were not in a favourable position in the event of attack, Carey more than once suggested to the prince that they should not linger but mount and return to camp. The prince, enjoying this eagerly-awaited, exhilarating experience of campaigning, indicated a wish to remain a little longer. Deciding that it was not for him to override the prince, Carey acquiesced. Suddenly from out of the maize burst a horde of Zulus firing their muskets and hurling their light-weight throwing assegais and vastly outnumbering the nine-man patrol. Carey – or was it the prince? – shouted the order to mount and ride for their lives, the prince rushed to his horse, put his foot in the stirrup – and the leather holster-strap gave way, tearing almost across its width to leave him dismounted as the Zulus rushed at him and Trooper Rogers, whose horse had bolted. Firing his revolver the prince fought bravely – so told Cetewayo later – until he fell pierced with seventeen wounds from broad-bladed, stabbing assegais. Rogers, too, fought to the death.

Riding hell-for-leather, stretched over their horses' necks, Carey and the others put distance between them and the Zulus before reining-in and realising that the prince and a trooper were missing. (Trooper Abel had been shot in the back and slid off his horse as he galloped away.) At once the enormity of the disaster struck Carey: this was no simple matter of a patrol attacked, but a tragedy which must affect his queen, the British and French governments and the commander-in-chief and could call into question not only the honour of the British Army but also his own personal honour.

The prince's death at once became a cause célèbre in Britain, in France, and throughout the Empire. Queen Victoria could not bring herself to utter Carey's name, Empress Eugenie was distraught with grief. The entire country debated. Was it Carey's duty to do his utmost to help the prince escape, even at the cost of his life? Ought he to have been last to gallop off – or was it a legitimate case of 'every man for himself' once the order was given? Had Carey shown himself to be a coward in saving his own skin heedless of an implicit duty towards the prince? In France Anglophobia raised its head: had this English officer deserted the Frenchman he was in duty and honour bound to protect with his life? These were perplexing questions I wrestled with and I was coming to understand that duty is a hard taskmaster. The verdict of Carey's court-martial cleared him legalistically but the stigma attached to him could never be eradicated. Better for him and Britain if he had died at the prince's side was the popular opinion with which I tended to agree. Perhaps fortunately for him, his life was to be cut short: he was killed a few years later in India, crushed by a military waggon that left the rails.

If any doubts remained in my mind as to an officer's duty they were dispelled once and for all when I read of Lieutenant Harward, accused of abandoning his men and riding off at speed while under attack from the Zulus. The court-martial acquitted him but the commander-in-chief, Sir Garnet Wolseley, although unable to reverse the verdict, refused to confirm the findings. Wolseley wrote: 'Had I released this officer without making any remarks upon the verdict in question, it would have been a tacit acknowledgement that I concurred in what appears to me a monstrous theory, viz., that a regimental officer who is the only officer present with a party of soldiers actually and seriously engaged with the enemy, can, under any pretext whatever, be justified in leaving them to their fate. The more helpless a position in which an officer finds his men, the more it is his bounden duty to stay and share their fortune, whether for good or ill. It is because the British officer has always done so that he possesses the influence he does in the ranks of our army. The soldier has learned to feel, that come what may, he can in the direst moment of danger look with implicit faith to his officer, knowing that he will never desert him under any possible circumstances. It is to this faith of the British soldier in his officers that we owe most of the gallant deeds recorded in our military annals; and it is because the verdict of the Court-martial strikes at the root of this faith, that I feel it necessary to mark officially my emphatic dissent from the theory upon which the verdict has been founded.'

With the Zulu Wars, the Kaffir Campaigns, and the Transvaal War of 1881 against the Boers read-up and more or less understood and digested I moved on to the South African War of 1899–1902 in which I had a special interest, for my father served in it. How he came to do so lay in family tragedy. My grandfather's untimely death in 1893 at the age of 48 sent his five sons and four daughters scattering from the big family house on The Square in quiet Market Harborough in Leicestershire to distant parts of the Empire: New Zealand, Malaya, Norfolk Island – that speck in the South Pacific Ocean – Australia, and Canada. At a stroke the sons became 'Empire-builders' – planters, ranchers, farmers – in the great Victorian mould. Never again would all nine meet together.

On the outbreak of the South African War the British government accepted the Dominions' offers to raise and send contingents to help fight the Boers. At once my father – then 20 years old – rushed from up-country to join the New Zealand contingent then forming only to find he was too late: it was already fully up to strength with volunteers. Undeterred, he took ship to Adelaide and enlisted in the Sixth Contingent Imperial as a private soldier, his regimental number 8, in the South Australian Mounted Infantry. In 1901 he was commissioned and commended for his 'coolness and courage in all circumstances' while serving in Field Intelligence with the Bushmen. The clasps on his medals – Belfast, Diamond Hill, Johannesburg, Orange Free State, and Cape Colony – guaranteed my reading of these and other campaigns, battles, and skirmishes so that for one in his early teens I had an unusually sound knowledge of the war as a whole and of the geography of South Africa. What was of absorbing interest to me, though, was the conduct of infantry regiments and their officers and men in battle: tactics, leadership, example, interpretations of duty.

It was not easy to graduate from small-scale African colonial wars to the First World War whose magnitude, and that of the slaughter, were beyond a boy's comprehension. Nevertheless, I devoured accounts of the epics of Verdun, 1st and 2nd Ypres, The Somme, Passchendaele, and the Hindenburg Line; names like Hill 60, Le Cateau, Delville Wood, Cambrai, and a hundred others became as familiar to me as that of Piccadilly Circus; and stories of aerial combat high over the trenches of the Western Front – Sopwith Camel versus Fokker Triplane – held me spellbound and I determined that one day, I would pilot my own aircraft.

These are the dreams that boys dream as they lie on the grassy bank beside a shallow, gently-flowing stream idly watching water-boatmen skimming across the surface, and scrabble with their fingers among the shiny yellow pebbles at the bottom for caddis-fly larvae in their cylindrical, twig-like cases of hollow stems and tiny stones. My dreams – fantasies, more like, that subtly shape the man – were based on my voracious, precocious, and indiscriminate reading of those true accounts of wars and battles and on adventure stories by the likes of Percy F. Westerman, the great G. A. Henty, who 'doubled' as war correspondent, and A. E.W. Mason. *The Four Feathers* made my heart swell with pride at the hero's courage in answer to the call of duty; and the Beau Geste books of P. C.Wren sent me to enlist, with countless thousands of other British boys, in the French Foreign Legion under an assumed name and abandoned nationality to become 'a soldier of France' fighting the merciless desert Tuaregs.

I could not have been older than 11 when Rider Haggard's hero, Allan Quatermaine, introduced me to the Queen of Sheba and King Solomon's Mines in the Mountains of the

Moon and John Buchan's *Prester John* carried me to the forbidding mountain fastnesses of Abyssinia, but by then I was already an experienced African explorer, intrepid companion successively of Doctor Livingstone and Henry Morton Stanley and trusted fellow-officer of Burton and Speke in our perilous quest for the source of the Nile. Nine years later I was to find myself real-life traveller in Abyssinia, following in the footsteps of my Victorian heroes.

Different causes may have similar effects. Family disaster scattered the seven sons and four daughters of the Haggard family from Norfolk to far corners of the Empire to earn their living at the same time that my grandfather's death sent his nine sons and daughters to those distant parts. For five hundred years in Pytchley in Northamptonshire, and later in Market Harborough, as husbandmen and ingenious countrymen ever-seeking richer yields from their land; as graziers when wool was king and entire villages were razed of their hovels for grazing land and their inhabitants dispossessed and cast out; as prosperous yeomen farmers and maltsters; and as landowners, brewers, and merchants Nunneleys had flourished and expanded their interests based upon the land and what the land produces. Each new generation built on past generations' enterprise and success; and strong religious beliefs were expressed in philanthropic concern for the poor, so that it might fairly be claimed that the history of the family over those five centuries is representative of English life.

The same claim might be made of the Haggards' squirearchy in Norfolk although their break-up was not due to the death of the head of the family but as a consequence of moving from 'trade' to country estate. They chose to forget that the origin of their wealth lay in trade shrewdly managed over several generations, and shut their eyes to the reality that the life of country gentlefolk cannot be sustained without substantial annual income. But for his father's financial miscalculation Henry Rider Haggard would not have found himself in South Africa developing his strong literary leanings and a knowledge of the Zulu nation so that his tales would come to enthral millions; and but for my grandfather's death my father would not have fought as an Australian in the South African War. The promise of a new life in a land coloured red in the atlas was as powerful an incentive to Nunneleys as it was to Haggards.

By the time I was 14, four of us had persuaded our headmaster, a brave man who had won the Distinguished Service Order in the First World War and whose experiences had caused him to turn to pacifism, to allow us to form a school Army Cadet Force unit so that we might begin to learn elements of the art and science of war and bring ourselves to a state of readiness for any military adventures which might lie ahead.

★ ★ ★

My posting, which despite my efforts I had been unable to prevent but to which I was in no way resigned, was to the 3rd/6th (Tanganyika Territory) Battalion of the King's African Rifles whose headquarters were at Dire Dawa. I was ordered to join a small, fast convoy of 15-cwt trucks which would depart Nairobi on 18 February and was due to arrive at Addis Ababa seven days later, depending on the reliability of the vehicles over many hundreds of miles of atrocious roads and tracks. There was also danger on the route. Bands of lawless shifta, armed to the teeth with captured British and Italian weaponry, roamed Abyssinia's border with Kenya's Northern Frontier District raiding, raping, and pillaging, and were not afraid to take on small, lightly-armed military convoys, especially under cover of night. Sentries must be posted at every halt; no vehicle may straggle or be left behind. These precautions were vital once the deserts gave way to the lush, green hills and valleys and forests of Abyssinia's Southern Highlands where ambushes could more easily be laid. Better to die fighting than be captured by the shifta and handed over to their women, whose merciless ferocity in torture and mutilation was a byword in these parts.

Our safari ran through places whose names were already legendary in the exploration of East Africa begun only a hundred years earlier: Thika, beside the Chania Falls, a traditional camping place since the 1890s of the East Africa Rifles and their successors, the KAR; Nanyuki, more than 6,000 feet above sea level, where the equator runs across the Nairobi road so that one can stand with a foot in each hemisphere; Nyeri, given its name by Lieutenant Richard Meinertzhagen of 3rd Battalion, KAR while on 'tribal pacifying duties' in 1902; past Mount Kenya with its glittering snowfields to Isiolo on the fringe of the Northern Frontier District. Isiolo's Indian dukas sold anything and everything a traveller to these wild parts might need and was the last supplies outpost in the southern area of the NFD.

A seven o'clock start each morning allowed the convoy to break the back of the day's journey before the sun rose too high. Mid-afternoon saw us laagered for the night, for it would be dark by six o'clock and camp must be set up, fires lit and the evening meal cooked, valises unrolled and camp beds slotted together. We slept under Africa's brilliantly-shining stars, woken only by the noise of sentries changing and the calls of wild, nocturnal creatures hunting their prey or shrilly losing their lives. Tomasi, I could see, was getting on well with the other servants, who were cheerfully helping him to learn his new job. Lounging with me on the bedding-rolls in the back of the truck as we pressed on northwards were Frank Bissley, a second lieutenant in the Oxfordshire and Buckinghamshire Light Infantry, and our two personal servants. We were unanimous that this was a far more comfortable way of travelling than in the lurching vehicles' cabs and it gave us also a grandstand view of multitudes of game: zebra, ostrich, giraffe, eland, Thomson's gazelle, bush-buck, and the occasional rhinoceros. The trucks kept well-separated so that none drove in the dense red dust-cloud trailed by those in front. Bissley, too, had been posted to 3rd/6th KAR and was resolutely determined to contrive a transfer to a British regiment. In no circumstances, he declared, would he learn Swahili as to do so would doom him to serve for the rest of the war with African troops. It was as well for his peace of mind that he could no more foretell the future than could the rest of us.

Beyond Archer's Post and across the Kaisut Desert's burning wastes Marsabit rose up tall and green, a huge area of forest and savannah and home to roaming elephant herds, then a long, slow slog over the Chalbi Desert before crawling up the steep escarpment that marked Abyssinia's border to Mega Fort perched at the top. Everywhere the detritus of war was strewn around: an Italian army ambulance lying on its side at the foot of a ravine, aircraft propellers spilling out of its shattered rear doors; a burned-out armoured car, abandoned in the Italians' retreat, with the motto 'Semper Pugnans' painted beneath a regimental crest; bombed buildings, abandoned fortifications. Stone-carved Fascist emblems – axe and faggots bound together – stood at the roadside as reminder of a fallen Empire. We camped beside the Awash River for the safari's last night beneath the stars and next morning drove into Addis Ababa. The town major billeted Bissley and me at the 'Albergo Imperiale', the city's best hotel now requisitioned as an officers' transit stop and staffed by Italians, to await a battalion truck from Dire Dawa.

Once the adjutant and Colonel Chalmers learned that neither Bissley nor I played contract bridge we were posted to Companies on distant detachment, Bissley to Captain Ionides' 'B' Company at Jijiga, between Harar and Hargeisa; and myself to 'D' Company near Mandera, a large village 40 miles from Berbera, British Somaliland's only port. In the six months that followed, Chalmers paid visits only to those of his companies strung out across Abyssinia and Somaliland which could make up a bridge four. 'D' Company being deficient in bridge-players I never saw him again following that first brief interview. I soon discovered that freedom from the Colonel's inspections was just one of many advantages of being on detachment.

I found the company encamped a quartermile from the prisoner-of-war camp it was guarding close to the main road running from Addis Ababa to Berbera. The rough scrub and 'wait-a-minute' thorn trees had been cleared for the askaris' Lines of long, grass-thatched huts, each with an extension tacked on to the end as African sergeants' quarters. On the edge of the beaten-earth parade ground stood the company offices with a flagpole in front of them. Set apart and a little distance away from the Lines were the Europeans' 160-lb Army flysheeted tents, the officers' tents pitched in a circle that was completed by a large mess tent. In the centre of the circle a log fire burned from sunset to sunrise to scare off the lion, hyaena, and jackal that prowled around during the night-time hours. This remote army outpost of Empire was exactly as my boyhood adventure stories had led me to expect and I was not disappointed.

I had arrived shortly before sundown and was at once directed to the company commander. With a smart salute I announced myself to the naked man squatting in a collapsible canvas bath outside the open flaps of his tent and sluicing himself down with the ubiquitous old canned fruit tin: 'Second Lieutenant Nunneley reporting for duty, sir.' Politely climbing to his feet Major Cox welcomed me with a wet handshake and an invitation to help myself to whisky from a bottle on a table within arm's reach of the bath while he dried himself. My life with the King's African Rifles had begun in true colonial style.

Tomasi had quickly furnished a vacant tent with my kit and prepared my bath and was now settling in with the other personal servants, whose grass huts were in easy shouting range of their masters. My new brother-officers began to emerge from their tents as darkness fell, and Major Cox, a Regular soldier who had risen from the ranks of the Black Watch, introduced me. They were a mixed bag: Pakenham-Walsh, captain and company second-in-command, had been a Shell Oil man in Kenya before the war; and the two subalterns I was now joining came from Scotland and Southern Rhodesia respectively, Scott of the Seaforth Highlanders, a lawyer from Morayshire, and Sinton, commissioned into the Argyll and Sutherland Highlanders. Sinton was still weak from a bad 'go' of cerebral malaria contracted while on blockading duty with his platoon at Zeila on the French Somaliland border and never fully recovered. Soon he would be invalided out of the

Army. It was from Zeila in 1854 that the explorer, Richard Burton, walked the 186 miles to Harar where as 'Haji Abdullah', a Moslem merchant, he was the first European to penetrate the 'Forbidden City'. Sitting in my safari chair, sipping 'Old Angus' whisky from a tumbler made from the bottom half of a beer bottle and warmed by the blazing fire, I passed on the latest news from England. I could see Tomasi chatting outside the servants' quarters, no doubt learning about the company and its askaris, and was sure that with his cheerful nature he would be getting on well with everybody in no time. The following morning I would take command of 16 Platoon.

It was the peacetime practice that officers and senior British NCOs were seconded, or 'attached', to the regiment for three-year tours of duty, reduced from five years. This dated from the earliest days of British East Africa, back in the 1890s, when the East Africa Rifles was formed. In this way the KAR was different from the Indian Army whose officers joined for their entire career. In wartime, too, we were seconded, not for any specific period but for the duration of hostilities. As a courtesy officers and British NCOs were permitted to wear their parent regiment's badges, buttons, and accoutrements except when ordered otherwise, when khaki safari tunic, shorts, and bush hat were worn with standard webbing equipment. This civilised custom was carried on in wartime except on active service in a war zone. It made for a colourful sight on such occasions as 'Retreat' with the lowering of the Flag when officers and British NCOs paraded wearing their varied head-gear – in 'D' Company's case the Black Watch bonnet, the Seaforths' glengarry, the Argylls' 'Balmoral' adorned with the British Army's biggest cap badge, and the rifle-green fore-and-aft forage cap of the Somersets. Pakenham-Walsh, the sole 'colonial', wore a bush hat with the Arabic brass 'sita' and black cockfeathers hackle of the 6th KAR pinned to a brown, diamond-shaped patch sewn to the brim.

The 3rd/6th was a first-line battalion raised in July 1940 and had played its part against the Italians. Now many of the 'colonials', officers and senior British NCOs who had led the battalion during the campaign, were leaving to return to their farms to increase food production and were replaced by 'Imperials' sent out from Britain. The result was a vital continuity as the 'old hands' passed on their knowledge of Africa and Africans. The 'Imperials' found the colonial way of soldiering at once freer and yet in many ways more demanding and carrying more responsibility than they had experienced in British infantry regiments. Leadership qualities needed to be developed and demonstrated to the full if the askaris were to have Europeans they would trust and follow into action.

The battalion was strung out from Dire Dawa with companies at Harar, Jijiga, Hargeisa, and Mandera. It was promised that guard duties would continue only until the PoWs were shipped out to camps in East Africa and elsewhere, and civilian internees repatriated to Italy. Down in East Africa second-line battalions would take over in order to release a division to fight the Japanese in South-East Asia. Intensive training was therefore interspersed with the task of keeping guard over thousands of prisoners. Almost all of the company's askaris were from Tanganyikan tribes. There were men of the Nyamwezi, lean and wiry; hefty, coal-black Wagogo from their arid plains studded with patches of jungle; pale, almost yellow-skinned, Chagga who farmed the lower, fertile slopes of Mount Kilimanjaro; burly Sukuma; a handful of lithe Hehe. From the south of the country and from Nyasaland there was a strong contingent of the Yao warrior tribe, some proudly bearing such names as 'Whisky', and 'Acland Acland' minus the hyphen.

A number of askaris had come from much further afield, from the Sudan and the West Nile; while Private Risasi had journeyed across Africa from the Gold Coast to enlist at Dar es Salaam. How Risasi came to undertake his great odyssey no European ever learned. He did, though, let it be known that his was a tribe which practised cannibalism , a revelation guaranteed to make him a figure of great awe and not a little fear in the company. Risasi claimed that in eating an enemy a man

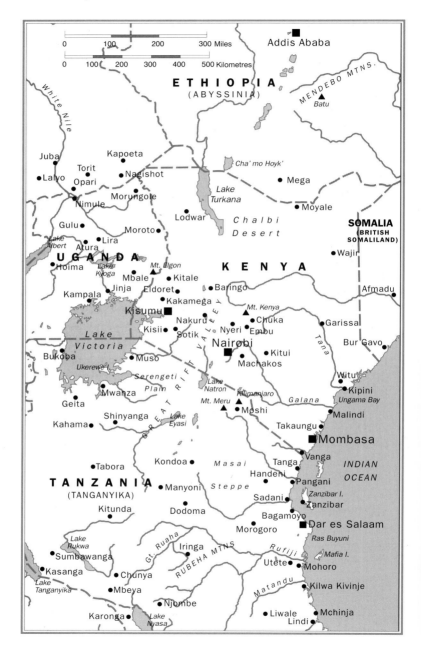

gained that enemy's strength. Fingers, he added, were the ten-
derest part of a man, while for sheer enjoyment the most succulent eating was the buttocks of a young girl. [Old customs –
and preferences – die hard: back in 1905 Meinertzhagen
recorded in his diary that a Manyema askari gave fingers and a
girl's buttocks a similar high recommendation.]

These were a cross-section of the thousands of tribesmen
who had taken 'Kingi Georgie's Shilling' when the Regiment's
Recruiting Safaris marched into their territories following the
outbreak of war with the promise of adventure, good pay, and
good food for all who came forward for Army service. Their
tribal lands were spread across Tanganyika, the Nyamwezi
around Tabora, the Hehe at Iringa, the Gogo in the Dodoma
area. Many were drawn in from their outlying villages to enlist
at Bukoba, Mwanza, and Musoma around the southern
shores of Lake Victoria and Kigoma on the eastern side of
Lake Tanganyika. Our askaris did not see themselves as mer-
cenaries and joined the Army to serve the distant, omnipotent
ruler who protected the remote rural peasant ways of life from
which the vast majority of them came. To many from impov-
erished tribal areas, where all too often only small quantities of
milk, blood, and beans were available, a powerful incentive to
enlist lay in the promise of regular meals including, especially,
a steady supply of meat. Perhaps, too, they reasoned that if the
'Serikale' – the Service – fed them there would be more for the
families they left behind. Young men who rarely had enough
to satisfy their hunger saw in the Army rations of meat, maize
meal, rice, beans, lentils, fruit and green vegetables, tea and
sugar a miraculous transition from want to plenty. High
above all these material advantages of Army service was the
intangible but immense, lifelong prestige to be gained by those
selected as askaris of the King's African Rifles.

A balanced diet combined with Army discipline and plenty
of physical effort made the askaris fit and strong and capable
of astonishing endurance in carrying heavy loads of arms,
ammunition, and equipment so that it was a rare occurrence
when a man fell out on the line of march. When a general

weariness and the fierce heat began to lower heads and hump shoulders there was always a bright spark, the platoon joker, who could be relied upon to raise spirits by breaking ranks with a rallying-cry as prelude to leading-off with the opening words of a regimental marching song, capering wildly as he did so. Up went heads, shoulders straightened, and in a moment every man was in full voice as the heavy infantry-man's 120 paces to the minute ate up the miles.

It is not easy to produce good soldiers from 'the rawest material in the world' as these recruits were labelled when they left their villages, yet they quickly and enthusiastically learned the infantryman's trade. By the time their basic training at Dar es Salaam was completed the use of the rifle, bayonet, grenade, Bren gun, mortar, and entrenching tool had – almost – become second nature to them. Life in a first-line battalion would hone their skills and turn them into real askaris of the KAR. Coinciding with my arrival in the battalion a new train-ing method called 'Battle Drill' had been imported from Britain and was now being introduced. This was a system of infantry tactics to be employed at ascending levels, from a section of ten men led by a lance-corporal to a platoon of thirty commanded by a junior officer, to a company of 150 men or more. The essence of the system lay in the word 'drill' – disciplined, coordinated actions and reactions in attack and defence situations. Executed principally by whistle, 'Battle Drill' was intensely physical, involving swift running to take up position, creeping towards the enemy under covering fire, deploying to form pincer movements, crawling, negotiating obstacles, attacking and charging with the bayonet. A great advantage of the basic system was that it could be put into effect whatever the terrain.

The company's routine was dictated by guard duty rosters at Mandera Camp, two platoons each 'on' for 24 hours and 'off' for 24 hours. Pitched immediately outside the main gate were two tents, one for the Duty Officer and the other for off-duty sentries. Inside the camp strategically-sited sentry posts gave long views down high wire fences separating the compounds. The Duty Officer was required to visit all sentries at irregular times during the day and night and to supervise their changing on a 'two-hours on, four-hours off' roster. There was always plenty to attend to during the 24 hours on duty, which occurred every third or fourth day depending on individual officers' availability according to the demands of training exercises. The New Guard took over at 7 a.m. each day, when Africa is cool and fresh, and were kept on their toes dealing with traffic entering and leaving the camp. Monster Italian trucks driven by 'trustie' PoWs brought supplies from Addis Ababa and Berbera, a steady stream of them halting at the main gate for the sentries to search for firearms and black-market food and tobacco. Intelligence officers from distant headquarters came to interrogate prisoners from whom they sought information; teams of International Red Cross observers arrived to check on conditions at the camp; and there was always the possibility of a single prisoner trying to escape or a mass breakout through a tunnel dug beneath the perimeter fence.

It would have beeen easy to relax vigilance. British Somaliland was one of those peacetime stations which had long been coarsely reviled by British troops because of its remoteness, the dry, fierce heat – up to 45 degrees Celsius – and its harsh landscape of scrub, sand, and lava rock. With the whole of North-East Africa except French Somaliland in British hands, there was scant chance of a successful escape bid; on the other hand, only 40 miles away lay Berbera where it might be possible to bribe an Arab dhow captain to sail across the Gulf of Aden – but the British were there also. Life in the prison camp seemed to appeal to the Italians, who gave little trouble, but it was safer to assume that escape attempts were being planned night and day and never to allow ourselves to be lulled into believing otherwise.

There was a special feature about Mandera Camp: it housed a thousand or so women and children interned after their army's defeat and the collapse of Mussolini's dreams of Empire and now awaiting repatriation under the protection of the International Red Cross. The presence of the women probably explained the camp's apparent harmony for there was no doubt that enterprising prisoners were finding their way at night into the women's compounds, and women into the men's. We reckoned that there were many more prisoners trying to get into parts of the camp than those who wanted to escape from captivity. The PoWs had found that silken bonds were stronger than barbed wire. There were persistent rumours that a woman could be had in exchange for a single tin of Nestle's condensed milk that mothers needed for their children, which may explain why this was the commodity most frequently discovered during truck searches. One of the favourite hiding-places was the 'well' beneath the seats in the driver's cab, capable of concealing two or three hundred tins and packages; another was between the huge fuel tanks and the chassis, difficult for searchers to get at. It was rare that contraband intended for the camp's black-market operators and to buy women was not discovered and transferred to the commandant's stores to supplement the women's and children's rations and it was intensely satisfying to see the barely-suppressed fury on the faces of the guilty drivers when their hoards were confiscated.

I had been with the company only a few weeks when trouble brewed up at the camp. A severe outbreak of gastro-enteritis brought tragedy, the death toll among the babies and infants quickly mounting and the Italian doctors unable to halt it. Day after day funeral services were held in the chapel followed by burial in the cemetery that lay beyond the wire. The mothers' anguish and despair, knowing that once they were repatriated they could never return to their child's grave, were heartbreaking to see. Some seemed to lose their reason altogether and spent every afternoon sobbing prostrate beside a small white cross in the broiling heat until friends gently persuaded them to return to camp. Tension between prisoners and the camp staff grew when stories circulated that the outbreak was due to the deliberate wickedness of the British in withholding drugs and a strongly anti-British atmosphere pervaded the entire camp. Matters were not helped when a lieutenant from Addis Ababa headquarters drove up to the Duty Officer's tent one morning and told me that British teams were visiting PoW camps to persuade selected prisoners to work for the Occupying Power. He explained that there was a serious shortage of the skills needed to restore Abyssinia's public services in major towns and technicians with relevant skills were needed urgently. Those prisoners who agreed to work for the British were promised good pay, good food, and comfortable conditions. I could see the logic of this scheme as it was the Italians who had brought the water, sewage, power plants, and other public utilities to the country both before and after their 1935 invasion and if there was to be a swift return to reasonable efficiency they were the best people to bring it about. Assuring me that he had the camp commandant's agreement to hold interviews in the Duty Officer's tent, the lieutenant produced a long list of the names and trades of the prisoners he wished to see. The first man to be brought in under escort listened with interest and after asking a few questions readily signed the Voluntary Agreement Form pushed across the table.

The second man had barely sat down before he jumped to his feet and with a contemptuous gesture made to leave. To my astonishment the lieutenant ordered my askaris to seize him while he himself grabbed the prisoner's hand and tried to force the thumb onto an indelible-ink pad as a preliminary to obtaining a print as evidence of acceptance of the offer. The Italian, a short, muscular man as broad as he was tall, took on the three of them, at the same time bellowing to the PoWs a few yards away inside the wire. Immediately scores of his comrades rushed to see what was going on. The uproar quickly became deafening as shouts and catcalls rent the air and enamel mugs were pounded on the barbed wire fence. The struggle continued, the tent rocking to and fro as bodies fell against its canvas walls, and still the Italian resisted. Refusing to take any part in all this I was, for the moment, merely a shocked onlooker. At last the thumbprint was obtained – but now the problem was what to do with its owner: he could not be allowed back inside his compound to warn of the British intention. The lieutenant ordered that he be bundled into a truck and taken for a drive in the bush. I refused to allow this and sent him under escort to a different compound.

I could not and would not stand by doing nothing in the face of such an outrageous breach of the Geneva Convention. I found it impossible to believe that a British officer could behave in this manner. Heedless of the uproar in the camp the lieutenant now ordered that the third man on his list be located and brought to the tent, and I could see that decisive action was imperative if a full-scale riot were to be avoided: as it was, things were almost out of hand. My problem was that as a second lieutenant I was junior to this madman and he therefore had lawful authority over me. To hell with him! Ordering the askaris to return to the Guard Tent I told the lieutenant that I would not allow him to continue and he must leave immediately. He refused, I demanded; he refused, I demanded. The battle of wills continued until he realised that he could not get the signatures or thumbprints he needed without our physical assistance and caved in. Ostentatiously making careful note of my name, rank, and unit, and promising serious trouble ahead for me – at the very least a court-martial for disobeying a superior officer – he climbed into his truck and drove off, still crimson-faced and panting from the struggle. The PoWs, meanwhile, were continuing a pandemonium that was growing worse by the minute.

In an attempt to pour oil on tempestuous waters I sent a message into the camp asking the compound's senior officer prisoner-of-war, Colonel Count Corsini, to come to my tent. After an amicable discussion we managed to satisfy honour on both sides but much damage had been done to the reasonably good relations that had existed and the commandant imposed a number of restrictions on the prisoners until relative harmony was restored. As for the mad lieutenant, I heard no more from him or any higher authority. If nothing else, the incident had graphically illustrated for me the difference between a lawful order and an unlawful one, and the right path of duty that every soldier must follow if his conscience is to be clear. This blot on our conduct as a signatory to the Geneva Convention was to have an unusual sequel: a picnic with the enemy.

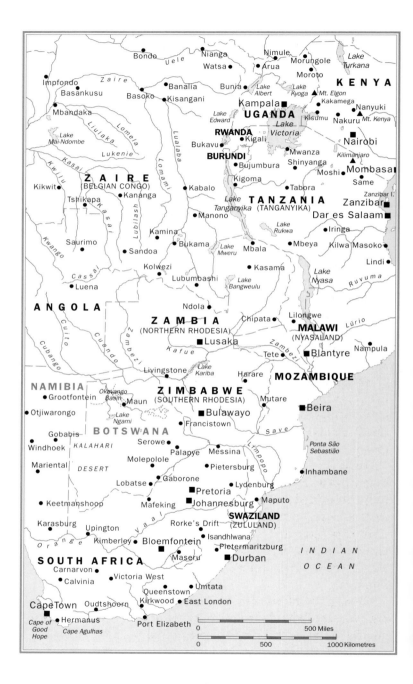

Despots and Victims

WITHIN THE THIRTY TRIBESMEN of 16 Platoon lay Bantu history of east and south Africa stretching back two thousand years, even beyond to the Stone Age. Unknown and unimaginable to my askaris, theirs was a story spanning centuries of wars of oppression and the assimilation of conquered peoples, mass migrations in ceaseless search of new lands to cultivate, and a thousand years and more of the slave trade whose victims had come to populate huge areas of the globe. A climactic point came in the nineteenthth century when European Powers descended on the continent to change forever its geography and its peoples' way of life.

The Bantu-speakers from West Africa began their migration at the time of Christ, moving further until they reached the southern third of Africa many hundreds of years later. This great mass movement had its origins in the discovery of iron, for it was iron that transformed the Bantu from their primitive state as hunter-gatherers to farmers of the land. From the central Benue River hinterland of what nowadays is Cameroun they pushed south and south-east into the forests of the Congo River basin, cultivating by 'slash and burn' and resuming their migration when the land was exhausted. With their iron spears they subjugated and absorbed tribe after tribe whose territory they entered, increasing their population as they did so. Centuries later they crossed the Zambezi River and turned eastwards to the fertile plains covering the high plateau to the East African coast before beginning their final, southward journey.

During the fifteenthth Century the Nilotic Luo from the region of the Bahr al-Ghazal tributary of the White Nile invaded what was eventually to become Uganda and Western Kenya and established themselves both north and west of Lake

Victoria. Two hundred years later the Luo and Bantu had merged and concentrated on the north-western shoreline and hinterland of Lake Victoria from the Nile to the Kagera River. A second invasion from the Nile created a Luo territory, forcing the Bantu to settle between the edge of Mount Kilimanjaro and two great rivers, the Tana and the Juba. The driving force which had made the Bantu cattle-keepers spread slowly but steadily east and south was a combination of hunger for land and an increasing population. Before the opening of the fourteenth century the migrants had crossed the Limpopo River; four hundred years later, now known as the Ngoni, they were established close to the south-east tip of Africa. Their nemesis was to be the Zulu King Shaka.

Shaka Zulu was one of the great figures in the history of Africa, a ruthless despot whose revolution in the art of war-making created empires which changed the face of the continent from its southern tip to central Africa. He realised that population growth which had carried the Ngoni to southern Africa represented colonisation too dense to be contained within the grazing lands of the coastal belt, and determined to bring them and their territory under his control before they could invade and absorb his tiny Zulu nation as they had invaded and subsequently assimilated others. He had inherited the war-making means to achieve his aim. Shaka was the heir of Dingiswayo, the great chief who instituted age-grade regiments to replace the tradition of puberty rites based on circumcision followed by a period of seclusion. Gone now were the days when war-making was more of a recreation with the opponents hurling spears and invective at one another before retiring when there were no more spears to throw. The newly-created regiments brought an important advantage to Dingiswayo, for they took away local chiefs' power and provided him with a disciplined standing army, a military machine over which he ruled supreme.

On succeeding Dingiswayo as chief of the Zulus in the early 1800s Shaka was in a position to bring into effect war plans which had been maturing in his mind. To the lightweight throwing-spear he added a short, heavy, stabbing assegai, or spear, to be used as a sword in the hand-to-hand fighting which he decreed must follow initial spear-throwing, ruling also that any man who discarded or lost his sword in battle did so on pain of death. The Zulu regiments were now trained to fight as an army, never again as individuals. Their battle-formation was the 'cow-horn' whose centre was a concentration of warriors and whose enveloping wings would attack one or other of the enemy's flank and even join together in an encircling movement. Advancing beneath an impenetrable carapace of giant cowhide shields, in the manner of the Roman legions' testudo, the Zulu with their new battle tactics brought deadly fear and inevitable defeat to those who attempted to stand and fight against them employing traditional methods.

Shaka's mfecane crushed all who stood in his path. In 1828 he launched a major offensive against the Ngoni people settled between Natal and the Cape Colony frontier. Such was his invincible military might that the Ngoni broke beneath the onslaught and fled to avoid extermination, beginning a long trek which over the next twenty-five years took them a thousand miles to the north, as far as the great lakes of Nyasa and Tanganyika. Fighting as they went, sometimes pausing for several years, the Ngoni adopted the military tactics that had brought such unparalleled success to Shaka. With this new power they defeated and absorbed most of the local populations they encountered, expanding their size and strength so that by 1835 they had crossed the Zambezi in force. In these years of warfare there were costly Ngoni reverses as well as victories, one such at the hands of the Sangu, who had survived by learning from the Zulus. The Sangu thrashed the Ngoni when attacked by them in 1856 and joined with the warlike Hehe so that, united by the fortunes of war, the two tribes settled in the area north of Lake Nyasa and were able, with their combined strength in numbers, to keep the hated Arab traders out of their lands.

One large Ngoni group trekked northwards again, this time

along the eastern side of Lake Tanganyika, taking many Nyamwezi captive as they did so and absorbing them within their population, and a second Ngoni group gained control of what was to become south-eastern Tanganyika. Shaka's mfecane, adapted by the Ngoni for their own survival, reached central Africa through countless wars and raids and introduced Ngoni culture to many peoples of different origins and cultures. Before the Ngoni descended on them the sole preoccupation of those who dwelt in the villages on the high East African plateau was with stock and crop-growing. The Nyamwezi were typical, growing millet, sorghum, yams, taros, manioc and sweet potatoes, with cattle-raising a fundamental in their lives. Stock represented power, wealth and social position and was used as currency as well as playing a major part in the life-cycle of birth, puberty, marriage, and death.

By the time dawn rose on the nineteenth century slaves had joined ivory as a commodity much in demand, bringing Swahili traders from the coast to the interior to compete with their established inland African counterparts. With slaving came raiding and outright warfare fuelled by the introduction of firearms. Adding to this, the Ngoni with their sophisticated military machine brought disruption to the plainlands until only the strong survived. Some nations adapted Ngoni methods and weaponry while others, wiser and with greater awareness that spears could not win against bullets, armed themselves with muskets. The strength of countless small kingdoms' relatively stable society was weakened steadily by bands of marauders who left their villages to engage in brigandage and warfare, and by slave traders and ivory-hunters who seized their human victims and traded them for ivory or sent them in chains to the slave markets at the coast. Heavily-armed gangs led by Arabs and Swahilis, also in search of ivory, added to the wholesale death and destruction which spread across the continent from coast to coast.

The Omani owners of the clove plantations on Zanzibar and the sugar-planters in the French islands of Mauritius and

Reunion needed a continuous supply of slaves, while the demand from Arabia was as strong as it had ever been. Such unrivalled commercial opportunity, coupled with the search for copper, sent Nyamwezi caravans westwards, deep into the heart of Africa.

This was the time also of the legendary slaver Tippu Tip, also known as Muhammed el-Murjebi, whose caravans comprised hundreds of Nyamwezi porters and gun-bearers. Tippu Tip would sometimes halt his caravan for months at a time, even two or more years if need be, when he found himself in a region containing a dense human population to be raided for slaves, or where large elephant herds could provide him with many tons of ivory. Tippu Tip's methods were simple and effective. He captured hostages whom he ransomed with ivory, so that people became currency: one young woman was worth one tusk. A major change occurred when firearms began to appear in quantity, making it even easier to capture slaves. The use of firearms for offence made it vital to possess them for defence, but in order to buy arms it was necessary to sell people as slaves – and the Nyamwezi sold their fellow-tribespeople without second thought. The economics of the trade changed again as flintlock muskets were superseded by one-shot rifles and when these in turn were replaced with repeating rifles their higher cost increased the demand for slaves with which to buy them.

Nyamwezi and Arab-Swahili caravans established themselves at Nyangwe and Kasongo, others at Tabora in Unyamwezi, 'the land of the Moon' to the south of Lake Tanganyika. Guns represented power in the competition for ivory and slaves so that it was not long before more guns and the ever-increasing demand for slaves encouraged a greater level of raiding resulting in population decimation and complete breakdown of village life. The over-supply of slaves, one result of the 1873 anti-slavery treaty, brought even greater misery and suffering as human life became cheaper than ever before. The more fortunate men and women surplus to requirements were those who became agricultural workers

47

and concubines for the dominant Yao and Chagga but the doomed majority were impressed into service as porters to carry the ivory to the coast. Those who fell by the wayside through sickness or exhaustion had their chains unshackled and were left to die, their loads shouldered by others still strong enough to continue on the line of march beneath even greater burden.

The Yao had adapted altogether too successfully to the changed times now dominated by Tippu Tip. In the past they had acted as middlemen for the kingdoms located in the southern Congo, exchanging mirrors and beads and fabric and other manufactured goods for slaves and ivory but now they concentrated on slaving and were soon the major procurers. For their part, the Nyamwezi had distinguished themselves as carriers as the only means of transporting goods, and built a monopoly by supplying porters for service with the caravans which made their way from the interior to the important markets of Kilwa on the coast, and Zanzibar. Further south, in the area of Lake Malawi, the Yao enslaved their own people for sale in Mozambique, while the demand in Brazil, too great to be satisfied from West African sources, brought Brazilian slavers around the Cape of Good Hope to buy for their country's plantation-owners. By the 1860s some 70,000 slaves were being exported annually from East Africa, while millions of others had already been exported through West African ports.

The abolition of slavery throughout the British Empire came in 1833, achieved at last by Protestants and Nonconformists united in determination, but did not become a reality for many years more; other countries were slower to prohibit slavery. In 1853 Britain asked Portugal to act against ships carrying slaves to the French islands in the Indian Ocean, in particular Reunion. Africans, too, were reluctant to give up their lucrative ivory- and slave-trading so that thirty years later it was clear that only a British administration in East Africa could bring slaving to an end, reduce famine, and halt the Ngoni invasions and war-making.

The Africa which until now had comprised a multitude of kingdoms changed again in 1884 when an international conference was held in Berlin at which fourteen European countries were represented. There were two items on the agenda: to clarify the state of trade on the Congo River and of navigation on the Niger River: and to attempt to define conditions under which future annexation in African might be recognised. The 'Scramble for Africa' had begun in earnest.

Territorial borders were agreed in Europe and the new countries within them proclaimed as protectorates and territories and given names by Europeans who had never set foot in Africa. Administrators, military forces, traders, settlers, missionaries, adventurers, and opportunists arrived in ever-increasing numbers to introduce and enforce stable government, sell manufactured goods and extract raw materials, seize and cultivate tribal lands, and strive to convert pagans to Christianity. By 1914 the partition was complete: seven countries had put into effect agreements reached in Europe so that in the entire continent only Liberia and Abyssinia remained independent. Italy, though, was already hungrily eyeing Abyssinia as a potential vassal state within her African empire.

In the East Africa Protectorate, annexed by Britain in 1895 and named Kenya, the British colonial administration's task was to introduce a white settler community, subordinating Africans and Asians to the European incomer. The government believed that the administrators whom they sent out were bringing the gift of law and order to peoples who had never known this benefit and should therefore welcome it, and was surprised when it was rejected. Enforcing this civilising policy cost thousands of African lives as the Kikuyu, the Nandi, and the Masai and other tribes strove in vain to prevent seizure of their most fertile lands for transfer to the Wazungu, the white men.

From the late 1890s until 1906 the East Africa Rifles and their successors, the King's African Rifles, sent out pacification and punitive expeditions. Their task was to impose and enforce law and order in aid of the Civil Power and bring to an end the continuous spear and bow-and-arrow wars fought between tribes, and between sections of the same tribe, always with cattle and women as booty. The Nandi in particular harboured a hatred of the white man which they did not trouble to conceal and continued to raid nearby tribes and attack mail-runners and their askari escort so that three successive expeditions of increasing size were needed before they could be driven out of their land for European settlement and resettled elsewhere.

Between 1901 and 1904 campaigns were waged by the King's African Rifles against another legendary African figure, the so-called Mad Mullah of Somaliland, and his followers, the dervishes, who had sworn to rid their country of Europeans. On both sides the casualties were heavy: in one expedition alone 2,000 dervishes were killed, with 34 British and African soldiers killed and 10 officers and 54 soldiers wounded.

In German East Africa the colonial government and settlers applied the harshest of methods to recruit labour for estates growing coffee, copra, groundnuts, cotton, and sisal. The seeds of widespread revolt were sown when the hut tax and other revenue measures were ruthlessly enforced, leading to renewed outbreaks of the violence which had greeted German rule from its beginning. A revolt by coastal Arabs fearing an end to their slave trade came in 1888; in 1891 the Hehe annihilated a German punitive expedition and for the next six years refused to submit; a military force had to be sent to the Tabora area in 1893 to chasten the Chagga and their Nyamwezi chief, Siki; the Ngoni were not crushed until 1897; and the Makonde in the Iringa region, led by the Yao chief, Machiga, held off the Germans until 1899. These uprisings were the forerunners of the last great revolt against the Germans, the 'Maji-Maji War' of 1905, whose origin lay in a German experiment in cotton-growing methods which was seen by African farmers as grossly unfair to them and taking priority over their food production. They protested strongly against the scheme and the brutality of the akidas, the overseers employed by the Germans, in carrying out their duties, who forced them to hoe for hours on government land for a few cents each week. If they paused in their work for more than a minute or two they were beaten with the rhino-hide whip, the kiboko, and prevented from cultivating their own shambas. This was exploitation practised on a massive, intolerable scale.

Enter Kinjikitile Ngwale, a mganga, a witchdoctor, thought by the Germans until they learned otherwise to be a harmless eccentric. Ngwale, though, was a man with a mission and possessed of a magical weapon of immense power. His mission was to unite people against the hated Germans and drive them out, and his weapon was a 'snake-spirit' that turned bullets to water. Word spread fast. From a hundred miles to the west and south chiefs converged on Ngwale's village to obtain the magic water and the seeds from which it grew for distribution to other people but still the Germans did nothing, confident that this was merely a little local difficulty which they would easily settle if it threatened to get out of hand.

As thousands of tribespeople of many different tribes and sub-groups prepared their cap guns, spears, and arrows for battle in the knowledge that bullets could not harm them the Germans' army of some six hundred askaris and no more than five hundred police remained at their bases on the coast. In the interior a handful of German non-commissioned officers commanding small detachments of askaris to enforce the law in a territory bigger than Germany had no warning of the rebellion which was uniting oppressed peoples in their hatred of the Ngoni, Arabs, and Germans who had invaded and occupied their land. Bedecked with millet stalks around their foreheads the rebels advanced on Samanga on the coast and in a gesture signifying defiance uprooted the hated cotton plants and set fire to the Arab trading-post. This they followed by laying ambushes for German patrols and firing more trade-posts, and burning alive a German garrison. The 'maji-maji' magic had worked its promised wonders: none of the rebels had been killed by bullets and the Germans had been driven out of the region. Weeks later an attack on another garrison yielded thir-

teen askaris dead without loss to the attacking force, this latest
success encouraging the rebels to advance on the main German
outpost at Mahenge in the Southern Highlands.

The governor had been forced into action when a war-party
speared and hacked to death a group of German missionaries,
so that the Mahenge garrison was waiting, ready for action, as
the columns of thousands of tribesmen appeared at the top of
the steep escarpment. Led by a mganga waving a millet stalk,
the attackers came under machine-gun fire at a thousand yards
but did not waver even as warriors fell. At shorter range the
German Schutztruppen askaris opened up with their repeating
rifles, the hail of fire stopping the attackers only when they
reached the thick defensive boma of thornbush several feet
high laid around the outpost's perimeter. The assault was a
partial success, with the garrison put under siege for three
weeks before it could be relieved.

The war had encouraged the Ngoni to join in against the
Germans who forbade slave-raiding and imposed taxes, and
now five thousand of them attacked the garrison at Songea.
Machine-gun fire mowed down hundreds of them and the survivors fled, leaving the Germans masters of the battlefield; the
magic of 'maji-maji' had been proved an illusion, a trick
played on a population steeped in superstitious beliefs. The
uprising was put down in ruthless fashion: the Germans created a famine by firing crops and entire villages in order to starve
the people into final submission, so that the silence of death
hung over the land. Chiefs were captured or gave themselves
up and were hanged: foot-soldiers were pardoned if they surrendered their pathetically inadequate weapons; and the last
groups of defiant rebels were hunted down and shot. The final
cost to human life caused by the famine was three hundred
thousand, so great a number that the entire region would never
recover from the loss of its population.

Eight years later the First World War saw Britain and
Germany as adversaries in German East Africa. Frustratingly
out-manoeuvred and out-generalled, and untrained in the art
of the guerrilla warfare waged so skilfully against them, the

British forces lost almost eight thousand askaris and more than four hundred Europeans in the campaign which ended with Germany's surrender to the Allied Powers. In addition, forty thousand of the quarter-million non-combatants enrolled for service died from disease. As part of the victor's spoils German East Africa was annexed by Britain and named Tanganyika Territory. Twenty years later sons whose fathers had fought against Britain joined the King's African Rifles to fight Kingi Georgie's enemies whoever they might be and wherever they might be found.

A Picnic with the Enemy

A QUOTA OF WOMEN INTERNEES was permitted to leave Mandera Camp twice a week for two hours to enjoy a change of scene and a stroll in the shade offered by the trees bordering a nearby nullah, a dried-up river bed. For their protection paroled military police, the *carabinieri*, were also allowed out of the camp. This concession was in addition to the mourning mothers' compassionate visits to the cemetery with so many tiny graves marked by small crosses. The commandant's decision was seen by some of us as humane and by others as foolish, for Somalia is well-populated with lion, hyaena, and other predatory animals as well as several species of poisonous snakes. That there were real dangers waiting in the bush had already been brought home to me. In the afternoon heat training was ruled out to allow all those not on guard duties to rest in their quarters until 4 o'clock. I preferred to take a walk at this time; sleeping in the daytime left me feeling sweaty and liverish and, in any case, once away from the camp I was free to muse over the immense solitude of Africa. I have always been something of a loner.

Meeting with the unexpected during these walks quickly taught me to be wary, more careful – and much better prepared for emergencies. One afternoon I found myself about to put my foot on a puff adder – its crescentic, bright yellow markings on a grey-brown body must have caught my eye in the nick of time – and I quickly leapt aside as it reared to strike. I remained motionless, knowing that the slightest movement on my part would encourage it to attack and fearing that without an antidote its poison could kill me in a few agonising hours. My clothes offered no protection: I was wearing shirt and shorts, knee-length stockings and boots with ankle puttees. And my revolver was not loaded. Perhaps the puff adder was replete and dozy after a meal, or perhaps it was my own split-second reaction that saved me, but suddenly lowering its head from the attack position it slithered away between the grassy tussocks. That lesson taught me to carry a personal 'snake outfit' of potassium permanganate crystals and a razor-blade so that if ever I were bitten I would at once slash the wound area to bring poisoned blood flowing out and then compress the crystals into the deep cuts. To help matters along I would employ my whistle-lanyard as a tourniquet. Even this prompt action would be no guarantee of success but might give me a sporting chance of survival, for there was no serum available in the wilds of British Somaliland and self-help was the only hope.

There are many species of viper in Africa, including mole vipers, puff adders, tree vipers, horned vipers, and the elusive Gabon viper, the most numerous and widely-distributed being the puff adder, *bitis arietans*, whose venom is a nerve poison which also breaks down the blood. Later I learned from Captain Constantine Ionides – 'Iodine', as he was generally known in the battalion – who earned international post-war fame as 'The Snake Man of Africa', that the puff adder's bite is rarely fatal to humans, although small children have been known to succumb to it. Had I possessed this reassuring knowledge at the time of my encounter I would nonetheless have latched on to the crucial difference between 'rarely' and 'never'. In my African apprenticeship I quickly learned to beware also the spitting cobra which can eject its venom over a distance of several yards. Should the venom enter the eye, temporary or even permanent blindness may result. Although the action is called spitting, it is due to compression of the venom gland driving out a trickle which is then carried on a blast of exhaled air. Spitting cobras were found from time to time in the company's kitchen garden by askaris working there but fortunately none was attacked; that experience fell to Ionides.

During another stroll I surprised a hyaena lying hidden from view in the long grass beside a thorn bush whose trunk offered a sliver of shade. Springing to its feet only five yards away and looking far bigger than I had imagined hyaena to be it faced me, hackles up and its great teeth bared in a fearful snarl as it stared into my eyes. If the hyaena was uncertain as to its next move, I was not and drew my .38 Smith and Wesson revolver with lightning speed; this time it was fully loaded with six rounds in the chamber. For long seconds we stared at one another before it turned and loped off in its ungainly way into the bush. The hideous beast, with its very yellow fur and black spots and drooping rear quarters probably weighed around 140 lb. Had it attacked me at such close quarters I would barely have had time for a single shot. It was another lucky escape. 'Experience teaches donkeys' and following that second, sharp 'bush lesson' I wore knee-length puttees for better protection against snakebite and armed myself with a loaded .303-in. Lee-Enfield rifle for my strolls, the belated wisdom of doing so confirmed a few days later when a young Somali girl was seized and carried off by a lion near her village less than a mile from 'D' Company's camp. My afternoon brushes with nature in the raw included me amongst those who questioned the commandant's wisdom in allowing the Italian women to leave the safety of the camp.

Early one morning three PoWs, one of them Colonel Count Corsini, approached the main gate and told a sentry that they wished to speak to his officer. By chance – or was it? – this was my day 'on' as Duty Officer. The camp's Italian officers, said Corsini, themselves enjoying feminine companionship, wondered whether their British counterparts might like to meet some pretty young girls? If so, perhaps a picnic might be arranged one afternoon? Thanking him for such unexpected consideration I told him that I would speak to my brother officers and let him know how we felt about his invitation, which he hinted was a 'thank you' for my refusal to allow the mad lieutenant to impress PoWs illegally into British service in flagrant breach of the Geneva Convention. It seemed prudent to keep the matter a close secret. The company commander could only veto the invitation out of hand in dutiful compliance with the strict rules against fraternisation with the enemy; and Scott had recently acquired a fiancee back in Elgin in Scotland and would be sure to turn the idea down. As I anticipated, Pakenham-Walsh and Sinton leapt at the prospect of a romantic interlude and I passed a message to Corsini accepting his kind invitation and suggesting the following Wednesday afternoon at three o'clock: the rendezvous would be a bend in a nullah a quarter-mile from the camp.

Corporal Abdulla, the Officers' Mess cook, packed haversacks with meat, bread, cheese, canned butter, sweet biscuits, fruit, tangy South African orange cordial, and Whitbread's beer and the three of us set out for the nullah in a state of pleasurable if guilty anticipation. Spread out on a tablecloth the picnic food looked fit for goddesses and very soon three arrived – lively, laughing girls of around 19 who ducked beneath the branches of the trees and introduced themselves as Olga, Gina, and a second Olga. At once they reminded us that the *carabinieri* threatened to shave the heads of women found fraternising with the enemy but the shadow this cast was a fleeting one for we assured them that Count Corsini and his friends had marked the *carabinieri*'s card and that they were safe with us.

The first hour was spent enjoying the picnic's delicacies and pairing off. Fractured Italian and English quickly broke down any reserve on the girls' part and the adventure was proving a great success until the curfew hour approached and Pakenham-Walsh decided it was time for a private conversation with his Olga. Pulling her to her feet he began to lead her half-laughing but protestingly towards a bend in the nullah. The other two jumped to their feet to rescue her and in a moment she had slipped from his grasp and all four of them dodged in and out of the bushes and thorn trees, three laughing and the fourth with a look of frustrated determination on his face. Sinton and I, who had no such immediate designs on the girls, lolled back on the rugs roaring with laughter until a furious Pakenham-Walsh at last gave up and the trio prepared to return to the camp.

As we watched them leave, their gay dresses flashing

through the scrub, we wondered whether there might not be something sinister lying behind Corsini's generous present. Why had the girls been offered in this free-handed way? Were they under instructions to find out from us details of military dispositions and strength in the area that might aid a mass escape? Moreover, if – as we were sure he had – Corsini had ordered the *carabinieri* to stay well clear of the picnic, knowing that in doing so he was authorising a clear breach of non-fraternisation rules normally so cruelly-enforced, there must be a stronger motive than a wish to give pleasure to three enemy junior officers. We began to realise that what had begun as a harmless tilt against spoilsport authority could take on the appearance of a serious security threat. No more picnics, we agreed, and earnestly hoped that we would hear nothing further from the Italians, or the British.

★ ★ ★

The risk of illness and disease is ever-present in the tropics and camp hygiene was strictly-enforced to maintain the company's fighting efficiency. The Lines were inspected daily by platoon commanders and the remainder of the camp by the Orderly Officer who checked the cooks and their kitchens, demanding that all utensils be laid out for his rigorous scrutiny. Pots and pans were scalded and scoured daily so that they shone as bright as the sun, drinking water was sterilised and fresh fruit and vegetables washed in a solution of potassium permanganate. In the paramount interest of hygiene the troops' latrines (cho) were sited a hundred yards away from the Lines; these were deep pits covered by a board floor in which circular 'squatting holes' had been cut. Protruding from one end of the pit was a woodfire which must be kept burning night and day by the cho orderly. Smoke from the fire was deflected into the pit and prevented from escaping by lids placed over the holes. Hot, dense smoke billowed out whenever a lid was lifted and flies, desperate to escape, hurled themselves at the bare bottoms poised above each hole.

It was early one morning, shortly before sunrise, when I woke with a griping pain in my stomach and headed for the officers' latrines along a narrow track through the bush. With each step the pain increased until the ground tilted this way and that and I fell on my face, unconscious. When I came to I found myself back in bed, an anxious Tomasi peering at me and patting my cheek. He explained that he had brought my morning tea at the usual time and found the tent empty. Later, when I still had not returned he set out to look for me and found me lying on the track in my pyjamas just a few yards from the cho. With the help of some askaris he had carried me back to my tent.

Somali dysentery is particularly severe, I was to discover, and in the days and nights that followed I frequently lost consciousness as red-hot knives twisted and turned and pulled in my guts. Much of the time I was only half-aware, lying in a bath of sweat as the sun beat through the canvas roof of the tent. God alone knew how high my temperature soared. Twenty, thirty times a day I struggled to the bucket Tomasi had placed inside the tent-flap. Often I was so weak and light-headed that I was only vaguely aware that he was lifting me on and off the bucket. From time to time blurred faces appeared in front of me and floated out of vision. Night and day became indistinguishable, and still bloody mucus flowed from me in searing spasms of agony that seemed only to increase in frequency and intensity. There was no British Army medical officer within two hundred miles, I understood in a rare moment of comprehension of what was going on around me, and an Italian doctor was brought from the PoW camp. He had no drugs, he told me, and his prescription was short and simple: I was to drink plenty of hot, sweet tea and this should prevent further dehydration. Notwithstanding the treatment the pains became even worse until I hovered in a nightmare dreamland from which I emerged only briefly and occasionally – was it when Tomasi gave me blanket-baths with lukewarm water? In those increasingly-rare lucid interludes I came to realise that I was now dangerously ill and growing worse by the hour. At last Major Cox did what he should have done days before and sent urgently for a British medical officer to come from Dire

Dawa with newly-available antibiotics which were still in short supply.

The doctor was shocked at my appearance and suffering, and voiced the suspicion that the Italian doctor's prescription might stem from a desire to punish the British for the camp's infant deaths. There was no doubt that, had the new antibiotics been more freely available, and supplies provided to the camp hospital, the mortality rate amongst the infants and babies would have been much lower. If I was indeed the victim of an enemy's revenge, which I doubted, I could understand his reasons if not his departure from the Hippocratic oath. Within a few days of taking a course of sulphonamide tablets I was on my feet again, rubber-legged and weak, deathly pale and as thin as a rake but mending fast thanks to my youth and a strong constitution. I was bitterly critical of Cox for his failure to act sooner, for if the other officers had not demanded that he send for British help I might have joined the children in the camp cemetery.

Tomasi had shown great strength of character beyond his years in the way he looked after me throughout my dysentery attack. Although I had only the haziest recollection of his nursing it was enough to tell me that he had earned my gratitude and that my instinct in engaging him was not mistaken. How many servants, of whatever age, I wondered, would have nursed their master as he had done, day and night for ten days on end? I would not forget the debt I owed him.

There were many other forms of disease in this remote area, some of which could seriously weaken the company's operational efficiency. In addition to the brothels in Berbera visited by our ration parties Somali women were available at the village of Lafaruq, 8 miles away. This easy access encouraged askaris to go on unofficial route-marches in spite of warnings and threats of pay stoppage for those who contracted gonorrhoea or, worse, syphilis. Prophylactics were available from the medical orderlies but few men drew them, and still fewer were deterred by explicit colour photographs showing hideously contorted and swollen male genitals. For the sufferers the treatment of ngonjwa ya bibi, which officers had to oversee, was painful to a degree. A catheter was inserted into the urethra and a solution of potassium permanganate fed by gravity into the bladder where it swilled around for a pre-scribed period before being discharged in the usual manner to the accompaniment of groans and clenched jaws. Another venereal disease was the chancre, the hard swelling which con-stitutes the primary lesion in syphilis and which grows larger and larger in the genital area until checked by frequent liberal applications of gentian violet. Notwithstanding the appear-ance of an infected man's genitals one had to conclude that there was no similar evidence of the woman's condition, or, if there was, then the driving urgency of physical need resulted in caution thrown to the winds. Perhaps the military dictum, 'It can't happen to me, it will be the man standing next to me who cops it', was made, with slight modification, to apply equally to sex risks as to battle risks.

There was continuous debate throughout the Army in North-East Africa as to whether or not medically-controlled regimental brothels should be set up for the troops. Those in favour argued that 'men would be men', and that when they were on military service far from the comforts of home it was sensible to give them access to clean women so that a unit's efficiency may thereby be unimpaired by preventable disease. Another strand of their case was that soldiers who nevertheless contracted venereal disease would not have used the official brothel and should therefore expect and receive rigorous pun-ishment. The opponents of controlled brothels argued that the British Army should not adopt the practices of decadent for-eign armies which catered for their troops in this way; and that the Church would exert overwhelming moral pressure to prevent their introduction. Those who suggested that regi-mental brothels might escape censure if they were confined to Occupied Territories – in this case Abyssinia and Italian Somaliland – were countered by the argument that it was the practice, not geography, that lay at the heart of the matter.

Had those whose views prevailed descended from their high

moral ground, and who doubtless enjoyed the pleasures of frequent sexual intercourse with their spouses, visited a VD clinic to see for themselves men in agonising pain they might – just possibly – have been moved to understanding and compassion. Few of the hundreds of thousands of soldiers in the East African Forces were Christians and Muslims; the great volunteer army was largely of pagans who found the white man's bewildering social mores thrust upon them for the duration of the war. I marvelled at their uncomplaining acceptance and could understand the strains they endured in long years away from home. Who could wonder when cheerful patience sometimes gave way to frustration that led to anger and outbursts of violence?

Apart from the pleasures and perils of consorting with the local prostitutes, entertainment for the troops had of necessity to be home-made. No touring parties of British entertainers, no mobile cinemas, found their way to Somaliland, and it fell to the occasional itinerant 'gulli-gulli' man with his snakes and conjuror's magic to enliven the day. The routine of guard duties and training could be broken only by calling on 'D' Company's own resourcefulness. The most-favoured solution was a ngoma. 'Ngoma' means 'drum' in Swahili and, in turn, 'drum' means 'dance'. Major Cox's announcement that there would be a ngoma in three weeks' time triggered intense activity which centred on brewing the native beer, pombe, from millet in sufficient quantity for 250 men determined to drink several 44-gallon drums dry. The brewing process required twenty-one days, hence the early warning which served also to give the organisers plenty of time to plan the great event.

Company Sergeant-Major Muliba recruited a panel of experts to assist him in producing a pombe worthy of the name; cows and goats were bought from company funds and herdsmen charged with bringing them to the ngoma's Head Butcher in perfect condition; and foraging parties went out to bring in sufficient wood to fuel the roasting fires which would burn from noon onwards on the great day. For every task associated with the ngoma there were volunteers a-plenty, and the sense of excitement which ran through the camp increased each day as bulletins on the pombe's satisfactory fermentation process were put out by the Head Brewer.

As soon as 'Retreat' was sounded and the flag lowered the askaris took over the company. The roasting, over two huge fires in the centre of the parade ground, had been going on for several hours and now smaller campfires were lit around the edges. A drum of pombe stood beside each of these satellite fires to save the revellers the effort of walking to a central point and in the gathering dusk the first drum beats began to throb, carrying Africa's captivating, mesmeric rhythms far across the Somali desert scrub. Discarding their uniforms in favour of animal skins and blankets the askaris wandered from group to group drinking the milky pombe from gourds and bowls, from Army Issue water bottles and glasses fashioned out of the lower half of beer and whisky bottles. Ritualistic courtesies were observed to the full with elaborate handshaking and formal greeting, military salutes were exchanged with tremendous verve and much foot-stamping. Led by self-appointed masters of ceremonies who would suddenly leap in the air as the mood took them and utter cheer-leading cries, chanting dancers joined the single file which slowly circled the blazing central fires. Those who left the long line to quench their thirst were immediately replaced by others so that there was never a pause in the dancing.

The feasting began as soon as the meat was judged cooked to a turn by the Head Butcher and his pishi assistants. In a free-for-all the askaris crowded around the carcasses hacking off gobbets and slivers of beef and goatmeat, often presenting favoured friends with a particularly succulent piece. Eyes grew wilder as the pombe took stronger hold and the singing and dancing and the quickening tempo of the drums carried the revellers back to the distant villages they had left so long ago. Throughout the ngoma the organising committee elected by their peers reigned supreme, in total control of the proceedings. This group had decked themselves out in clever copies of senior British officers' uniforms complete with red band around a makeshift peaked cap and red-and-gold gorgets at the collar. Each had chosen his rank or been given it by the 'General Officer Commanding Ngoma'. 'Colonels' and 'Brigadiers' stood authoritatively in front of 'Ngoma HQ', each with his own sphere of responsibility, dispatching runners to the cooks, the butchers, the woodcutters, and the brewers. Cracking salutes were exchanged between these senior officers and their subordinates whose situation reports were received with grave dignity.

The company's officers and British NCOs had been invited and joined in, wearing the most casual dress we could find in our kit; as a compliment to the 'GOC Ngoma' we had decided that none of us would wear badges of rank that night. At once we were drawn into the line of swaying, stamping dancers endlessly circling the fires whose tall flames leapt into the night. As fresh fuel was thrown on a million sparks rose in clouds to murmurs of approval from the drinking onlookers who knew a good fire when they saw one. From time to time a Mzungu would leave the dancing to join a small group of askaris for a chat, his pombe glass kept well-filled by an attentive orderly detailed for the purpose by thoughtful hosts. The warmth of the askaris' hospitality knew no bounds as they cut off a particularly succulent chunk of meat and with a courteous smile offered it to a European as a mark of friendship and equality between men bound together in service.

Drinking and eating the endless supplies brought to the fringes of the ngoma the askaris gossiped happily together, inviting passing friends to join them for a while so that groups continually formed, dissolved and formed again. As the night wore on even the drummers began to tire until the last beats sounded and silence fell over the camp. Dawn revealed a battlefield after the battle. All around prostrate bodies lay motionless until the warmth of the early sun encouraged numbed brains and stiff limbs to begin to stir and one by one the hung-over soldiers drifted back to their Lines for a hair of the dog that bit them and a critical review of the night's events.

Back in their villages, long after winning 'Kingi Georgie's' war for him, old men would tell the story of their ngoma in the far, far beyond.

It is always Life's capricious way: after the pleasure, the pain. As dawn broke one morning just a day or two later I drove into Mandera Camp on a routine check inspection and was horrified to see a rifle leaning against a sentry-box and no sentry in sight. For a moment I feared the sentry must have been seized in a mass breakout attempt. Then I saw Private Sumani was fast asleep in his box, so dead to the world that the noise made by the truck's engine had not wakened him. Removing his rifle I put it in the truck before shaking him awake and placing him under arrest. At the company office, Army Form 252 charged Sumani with his crime: that he, whilst a sentry, had been found asleep at his post. Later that morning Major Cox held company 'Orders' at which defaulters were brought before him. Private Sumani was marched in under escort by CSM Muliba and the charge read out. I stated the circumstances. Asked whether he had anything to say he simply acknowledged the offence. The company commander announced the punishment: twelve lashes of the kiboko, the rhino-hide whip used in the KAR in cases of serious crime. New to Africa and the ways of the regiment I had not known that flogging was carried out, nor that it had been a form of military punishment since the earliest days of the East Africa Rifles, before the turn of the century.

At noon three platoons and all available company head-quarters personnel – drivers, signallers, cooks, orderlies – were marched on to the parade ground by their platoon sergeants to form three sides of a square. The platoon commanders then marched on and took up position in a row five paces behind the company commander so that the officers completed the square. A heavy silence fell. Had a pin been dropped on to the sun-baked earth it must have been heard by all on parade. In my mind's eye I pictured Captain Dreyfus being disgraced by the French Army. I was appalled by what I was about to witness. The Union Flag hung limp from the flagpole, the regimental flag from a jackstaff. A small dust-devil formed and went twisting and swirling across the parade ground in a sudden, thermic surge. CSM Muliba marched on, five paces ahead of two askaris carrying a triangular wooden frame with wrist and ankle straps hanging from it. The kiboko in his left hand and swagger-stick in his right, he barked out an order and a sergeant and escort marched forward with the prisoner already stripped to the waist. Private Sumani was ordered to lie across a bulky, grass-filled sack and straps were fastened so that his wrists were at the apex of the frame and his ankles to its wider base. Another order followed and the sergeant took the kiboko from CSM Muliba and passed it to the corporal detailed to administer the flogging. Sumani's escort swiftly removed his trousers and laid a leather apron across his back to protect vital organs.

In this nightmare military ritual performed with elaborate, slow-motion choreography Major Cox read out the charge and his sentence, then nodded his head. Muliba saluted him and called out an order. Kiboko in hand Corporal Juma stepped forward to calculate the distance needed to ensure that the strokes would fall accurately on Sumani's bottom and nowhere near the kidney area, then waited at attention. Now Company Sergeant-Major Spalding gave the order for the punishment to begin; in accordance with KAR custom the African sergeant-major would loudly count each stroke in Arabic. The first lash sounded like a sharp pistol-shot. Then a second, a third, a fourth, a long, breathcatching pause between each one. All 120 men on parade, Europeans and Africans, stared with fascination as Sumani's bottom broke into a mass of dark red, criss-crossing weals; it was as though every one of us was suffering with him, willing him to bear it. With each stroke he flinched but made no sound. At last, at last the twelfth had fallen. In a moment the straps were unfastened and Sumani was on his feet. Again in accordance with custom he turned towards Major Cox and gave a smart salute before being escorted off the parade ground by two medical dressers with their first-aid panniers. That evening I went to the Lines to see that he was as comfortable as he could be and excused him duty for two days. His stoic acceptance of the ordeal and his courage had won the admiration and sympathy of the company. I hoped I would never again have to witness a flogging, let alone be instrumental in causing one to be administered.

One night two years later, in his frontline slit-trench in the Burma jungle, a signaller fell asleep on sentry duty allowing the Japanese to slither through the defensive perimeter and penetrate the Battalion Headquarters Command Post. For this crime, committed in frontline conditions and ranking with desertion, showing cowardice in the face of the enemy, and casting away arms in the presence of the enemy, the penalty is death by firing squad.

★ ★ ★

In 1951 leaders of the Mau Mau rebellion, which although eventually suppressed hastened Kenya's independence, gave themselves high 'military' rank, several of them assuming also the names of favoured Communist countries. This adoption of a military-type command structure may have been inspired by a 3rd/6th KAR ngoma. Waruhiu Itote, 3rd/6th KAR's wartime officers' mess corporal at battalion headquarters, and one of the handful of Kikuyu in the battalion, styled himself 'General China'. Other 'Generals' included 'Tanganyika', captured and hanged; and 'Abaswein', captured. Dedan Kimathi, Mau Mau's overall leader until he was killed in a shoot-out was 'General Russia' before promoting himself to 'Field Marshal' in command of 'Land Freedom Armies Command'. Waruhiu was capable and well-liked in the battalion. As President of the Mess Committee in Ceylon I had daily dealings with him; and Ian Sinclair, whom I succeeded as adjutant during the campaign in Burma, taught him to handle the Sten gun as a self-defence weapon should the Japanese penetrate our perimeter. Every man-jack fought if need be and certainly, when battalion headquarters was attacked by Japanese night-raiding jitter parties, there were no non-combatant duties.

From the late forties Waruhiu became involved in Mau Mau, and when the Emergency was declared headed a gang which operated in Mount Kenya's forests. It was in these forests that he surrendered in 1954 and was imprisoned. Sinclair, who had resumed his profession as a banker in Kenya, told the government of his personal knowledge of 'General China' and suggested that Waruhiu might be willing to talk to him. Back came the answer: 'He is singing like a canary and we can hardly keep up with what he is spilling to us!' Regarded as a patriot and hero in the independence struggle nonetheless, Waruhiu was rewarded by President Jomo Kenyatta with appointment as second-in-command of the National Youth Service, a voluntary organisation which does public works – a type of non-military outfit uniformed, housed, fed, and paid by the government. In two autobiographical volumes this former soldier of the KAR and Mau Mau leader praised the commanding officer and the other officers of the battalion for their conduct in Burma; for his part, we who knew him can testify that he earned his Burma Star campaign medal. Waruhiu Itote died from natural causes in 1993, a death denied another former 3rd/6th KAR askari, Juma Ndolo, nine years earlier.

When I first knew Ndolo he was our battalion storeman. That was in Abyssinia, in 1942. Through merit, strength of character, and courage, he moved up through the ranks to corporal, sergeant, and finally to company sergeant-major. In the immediate post-war years, when it was policy to 'Africanise' the KAR, Ndolo became an 'Effendi', a platoon commander, before going to England to attend an Officers' Training Course at Mons Barracks. Shortly before his country's Independence he was awarded the MBE for bravery and eventually became commander of the Kenya Army with the rank of major-general. In the early seventies General Ndolo was believed to be privy to a plot to oust President Jomo Kenyatta and was retired to his cattle farm as punishment for not revealing the existence of the suspected conspiracy. On 6 April 1984, aged 65, he died in a car accident on the Nairobi–Mombasa road, on his way to the wedding reception of his son at Sultan Hamud. Was it an accident, or something more? Fatal car accidents that befall prominent persons have earned for themselves something of a sinister reputation.

Their service with the KAR had developed the qualities and powers of leadership of these two remarkable men, Waruhiu Itote and Juma Ndolo, who saw their duty to their country in diametrically-opposed ways. Former Mess Corporal Waruhiu, 'General China', claimed that he learned military tactics and discipline when fighting the Japanese in Burma; and General Ndolo most certainly had done so. It was a strange coincidence that the two of them, one a Kikuyu, the other a Kamba, and both from Kenya, should have served in the Tanganyikan 3rd/6th Battalion.

The Last Roadblock in Africa

THE COMPANY'S RATIONS were drawn twice a month from Army stores at Berbera, 40 miles away, when a fatigue party with one 15-cwt truck and a 3-tonner made the trip under an officer. Our diet was well thought-out and suitably varied: maize meal for the askaris' staple food, posho, with fresh meat and vegetables supplemented by fruit from the Cape and Kenya for all. Perhaps to compensate us for long months spent in Somalia's blazing deserts the Europeans' rations sometimes included six bottles of beer and one of whisky per man per month. Once the trucks were loaded and under guard there was time and opportunity for a few hours' relaxation before returning to Mandera in the late afternoon. The fatigue party made off in search of women and drink, while the officer could visit the local mess to luxuriate in a proper, full-length bath, then go on to the Somaliland Camel Corps' house to pick up more gossip and rumours. With luck he might meet up with Somalia gendarmerie officers making a rare trip to Berbera.

Junior officers seconded to the gendarmerie were appointed 'Bimbashi'. This grand title carried with it no extra pay, only a glittering, oversized crown-and-star combination worn in place of the regulation badges of rank so that at first glance the wearer appeared to be a lieutenant-colonel in the Ruritanian Army. I was glad that I had not been sent to the gendarmerie for it was the fate of many of its officers to be posted with their platoons to keep inter-tribal peace in Italian Somaliland's most remote areas, often to garrison Beau Geste-style forts for months on end and with no other European within a couple of hundred miles. Not surprisingly, a good many Bimbashi turned to drink in their enforced solitude; cheap, rotgut grappa was the only liquor available in quantity. Others took local women as concubines, a risky business as Somalis are fiercely jealous of their womenfolk and all too readily resort to the bilal, the dagger, to satisfy their honour. The attractions of satisfying sexual urges had therefore to be balanced against the dangers of provoking unpredictable and volatile men into violent acts of revenge.

Despair which turned to madness took its toll of gendarmerie officers in their isolation. Commanding 'the most difficult, proudest, vainest, most merciless, and friendliest of men', as they have so aptly been described, whilst patrolling thousands of square miles of rock, scrub, and desert in often fruitless attempts to prevent tribal wars caused taut nerves finally to snap, both in those lonely fort-outposts and on safari showing the Flag. The first signs of approaching crisis could appear in simple forms, perhaps in not bothering any longer with proper meals but picking with a fork from a bully-beef tin, going unshaven for days on end, letting the hair grow long and bushily unkempt and generally 'not bothering'. At a later, potentially more dangerous, stage the lonely man could find that he was talking, talking, talking to himself – and enjoying this interesting companion who so much agreed with his opinions. As weeks turned into yet more months of loneliness the victim might develop the paranoid obsession that the forces of evil were about to overwhelm the forces for good. This growing conviction could be 'proved' by listing alternately in two columns – one headed 'Evil' and the other 'Good' – the serial numbers which newspapers print at the top of each day's front page, any stack of old newspapers serving the purpose. Invariably the total in the 'Evil' column would be found to exceed that in the 'Good' column, thus making it a certainty that the world was about to fall forever into the hands of Satan. Endless adding-up in the increasingly frantic but vain hope that an error had been made and the world saved became so urgent that sleep was an unbearable wasting of vital time. Burdened with the weight of such dreadful, inescapable knowledge of the imminent fate of mankind there was nothing else to do but end it all with a pistol-shot to the temple or up through the mouth. One desperate officer made certain-sure with a burst of automatic fire to the head. At least seven of the gendarmerie committed suicide and were recorded as 'Died on Active Service'.

I came across this mental condition a couple of years later. A brother-officer, Lieutenant Favell, a somewhat elderly reinforcement to the battalion – he must have been 30 – who joined us during the Burma campaign was reported to me shortly after dawn one morning as having gone mad and about to shoot himself. I was then the adjutant. I went to his tent as though making a casual visit and found him distraught and wild-eyed as he added-up his two columns of figures taken from the airmail issues of the *Daily Telegraph*. A loaded revolver was on a chair beside him.

'There's no doubt about it', he shouted, 'Evil has triumphed! We're all done for!' This 'opener' allowed me sympathetically to suggest that the totals might be checked by the Quartermaster, a man known by us to have a love for accurate figures in his Army inventories, and after a long debate Favell finally agreed. For the time being at least his suicide was avoided. Later, when I visited him in hospital I found that he had crammed newspaper under the door and around the frame and also around each window of his room in order to prevent invasion by those all-conquering forces of Satan. In Favell's case it was not months of utter loneliness but corrosive self-doubt that had sent him toppling over the brink. We never saw him again; he was not of fighting material and should have been posted to a worthwhile job with 'the boys in the backroom', not to a first-line infantry battalion.

For the Bimbashi there were other perils lurking besides those associated with drink and women. Somali troops had the reputation of lacking the self-discipline, and acceptance of discipline, which must be the first essential in military service, and no more so than in combatant units. Rumours of near-mutiny or at the very least unrest were persistent and officers kept the closest of eyes on their men at all times. It seemed inevitable when a Bimbashi was reported murdered in his bed one night, near Cape Guardafui, an axe driven into his chest with such force that it went also through the mattress beneath him. Whether he had slighted one of his soldiers or had taken another man's woman was never discovered for no Somali would speak to the feranji against another of his tribe.

I had come into Berbera with the ration party, bringing Tomasi with me to enjoy a change of scene, and was lounging in the mess overlooking the harbour when an explosion boomed and flames and black smoke mushroomed from a petrol-laden dhow moored eighty or so yards offshore. Minutes later a second dhow went up in exactly the same way. Anchored close to the blazing vessels lay a large schooner, the *Bushire*, also with a cargo of petrol. At once the alarm sirens sounded and all available troops were ordered to the beach to save the schooner's cargo while the dhows were allowed to burn to the waterline and sink in the shallows. A chain of men waded out from shore to ship to off-load the fuel hoping that she wouldn't go up in a fireball which would engulf those on board and in the water closest to her. Hundreds of tins – debes – were passed over the side to our human conveyor-belt until all the petrol was safe on dry land. Investigators shrewdly concluded that the fires, which mirrored others occurring at that time, were caused by sabotage.

There are many who believe the desert war was won by the ubiquitous debe which fuelled the armoured and soft vehicles that fought from the Western Desert to the Horn of Africa. The standard 44-gallon drum was born of ten 4-gallon debes, whose name derives from East Africa's earliest coffee harvests, when pickers were paid by the debe, and today's 4-gallon iron coffee measure is the debe's descendant. Certainly the debe has a noble history. In the opening years of the 1890s paraffin played an important part in the lives of British East Africa's settlers and the brightly-shining tins it came in were subsequently used as containers for anything and everything. The debe was vital for the carriage of water to the home and on the farm but it had also many unexpected and ingenious uses. Flattened out, it was building material for roofing and walls;

hammered, it could be turned into baking and roasting tins; and punctured with nail and hammer a pair of debes could be fashioned into a refrigerator using charcoal through which water was filtered into a cooling-chamber containing meat suspended from a hook. Debes became ovens when hung above a burning fire and in her book, *The Kenya Pioneers*, Errol Trzebinski tells that an ingenious mpishi could fashion a jelly mould or a soufflé dish from a debe. In skilful hands the debe's versatility knew no bounds.

Life was by no means hard for those stationed in Berbera, in many ways as remote and paradisal as Shangri-La. Because it was a receiving port from which supplies were sent forward to units in the interior few senior officers bothered to visit it, leaving the 'locals' free to sit back and enjoy themselves without irritating interruptions by busybodying brasshats. Crates which broke open accidentally or by design on the dockside or in the depots became 'first pickings' for those on the spot, so that a brigade commander's champagne was unlikely to leave Berbera if the cases were labelled accurately. It would have been safer to mark such agreeable consumables as 'Training Manuals' but the consignors never learned this basic lesson and Berbera's 'base-wallahs' enjoyed a lifestyle inappropriate to their rank while the consignees fumed impotently at the port staff's gross inefficiency.

Berbera provided other exotic luxuries for those who had the taste for them. Back in 1854 the explorer, Richard Burton, described the Somali orange-seller girls at the ford outside Harar, with their regular features and perfect figures, as the most beautiful in the world and a hundred years later the charms and easy grace which had delighted him so long ago were to be found also in Berbera. It was a simple matter to requisition a house in the Arab Quarter and furnish it with proper beds to be warmed by willing Somali or Arab girls, so that few members resident in the mess actually slept there. On an occasion when Tomasi and I overnighted at the mess we found ourselves in sole possession, the regular members having melted away after dinner. I suspected that down in

Kenya there was a thriving black market in postings to Berbera-by-the-Sea, the Horn of Africa resort offering delights of the senses and of the flesh and none of the tiresome discomforts of active service in the field.

Pakenham-Walsh suggested that he and I might take a weekend's leave based on Berbera, where the Camel Corps house was available to officers of other units. His idea was to spend the daylight hours walking in the green pastures around Sheikh Pass, a cooler place in the hills some 50 miles away, and return to Berbera to sleep in the Corps' house. The proposition seemed an attractive one but he kept it dark from me that he had a weightier matter on his mind for which he needed an accomplice. We found the house set deep in the heart of the Arab Quarter with its narrow streets running down to the sea. All the dwellings were two- and three-storey, their terraced flat roofs bordered with parapets high enough to serve as breaks against the kharif, the hot, strong westerly wind which blows in the daylight hours from March to December to create blinding sandstorms until abating in the evening. The house was complete with a resident Arab housekeeper-janitor, Ali, who used and misused it as he wished unless officers were staying there, when he acted as major-domo and bossed the personal servants, orderlies, and cooks they brought with them.

The luxury of sipping cool drinks on the roof while gazing out across the Gulf towards Aden as lateen-sailed dhows headed for the shore and dusk turned to night awakened Pakenham-Walsh's romantic imagination and my own. At his clap of the hands Ali appeared, dressed in a white gown to his ankles and with an embroidered cotton cap on his head, for all the world a figure from the 'Arabian Nights'. 'Bring two beautiful dancing-girls', commanded Pakenham-Walsh, and with a half-bow Ali withdrew, soon to return with a pair of little girls who could not have been older than 9 or 10. It was clear that Ali knew Camel Corps officers' preferences but theirs were most decidedly not ours and the girls were sent away, no doubt puzzled by their abrupt dismissal. Satin-skinned Fatima and Aila, both of them tall and elegant and each with a houri's hourglass figure and long, black hair falling to the waist, their eyebrows like twin crescents of the moon, entertained us with dance and soft, murmuring song beneath a perfect canopy of stars until the eastern sky lightened with the first rays of the sun rising beyond the Gulf. The following evening they returned to while away the hours with us and again left with the dawn.

Within a day or two of these dream-like nights came news that the repatriation of civilian internees was now imminent. Two famous Italian transatlantic liners, *Rex* and *Italia*, sailing under the protection of the International Red Cross, were due to arrive off Berbera a few days later to embark 9,000 women and children, nuns, the chronically sick, senile, and mental defectives of the 34,000-strong Italian colonist population in North-East Africa. More ships would arrive over the coming weeks. From camps in Abyssinia, Eritrea, Asmara, and Mandera convoys of motor vehicles would carry the internees to the port over a four-week period. In order to detect and recapture escaping prisoners-of-war a chain of seven roadblocks would be established between Addis Ababa and Berbera. 'D' Company was to provide one officer and a platoon to set up and man the seventh and last roadblock. It was inevitable that Major Cox would assign his latest arrival to the task and I prepared 16 Platoon to leave on detachment.

For the block and the platoon's camp I chose a point halfway between Mandera and Berbera, where the road came round a low hill before dipping to cross a narrow culvert over a nullah and ascending a rising curve. Although without any signs of habitation it was shown on the large-scale map as 'Santala'. I reasoned that the convoys would see the block only at the last minute, so that any fleeing PoWs in the vehicles would have no time to jump off and run into the bush to make a loop and rejoin out of sight further along the road. Sentries posted on the low hills would watch for any evaders. The site had other advantages: the hills would give us some protection from the early morning and late afternoon sun; and the nightly temperature-drop would cool the sand in the nullah-bed.

We would live for the next month in this burning lunar land-scape of sparse light scrub, sand and lava rock. To assist me battalion headquarters sent Sergeant Lapthorn, a Regular soldier who had served in a British infantry regiment before his wartime secondment to the KAR. Between us we devised a system whereby each convoy would be halted by the African platoon sergeant a hundred yards from the block and guarded by sentries posted at intervals along the road. At a signal four vehicles would come forward for examination. As each pair was cleared they would drive off and another couple would join the two still halted at the block so that a reasonably smooth, continuous flow should be achievable. In making our checks Lapthorn and I would 'leapfrog' one another through the convoy until the last vehicle had been sent on its way.

I decided that on boarding the vehicles we would go to the internees sitting at the rear and work our way to the front, looking straight into the face of each one as we asked in Italian several set questions I prepared, such as: 'Where were you born?', 'What is your mother's name?', 'What is your father's name?' and 'What is your date of birth?' By scrutinis-ing each person and asking questions which must be answered I hoped that this procedure would enable us to spot any disguised PoW who had passed successfully through other roadblocks in the chain. I was determined that no escapee should make the voyage back to his homeland. The well-rehearsed system worked well in practice when the first con-voys began to arrive at the roadblock. Trucks of all sizes, buses, and ambulances had been pressed into service to oper-ate a long-distance 'shuttle' so that as the internees were de-bussed at Berbera the empty vehicles turned round and headed west to bring another load of passengers several days later.

Berbera harbour was too shallow for any but dhows and vessels of similar draught to enter and the two great liners, the pride of Italy's mercantile marine, with their distinctive, sharply-raked bows, lay offshore waiting to receive the intern-ees carried out to them by relays of lighters. It was not difficult to picture the emotions of the colonists who were about to

77

return to their homeland after years away making a new life in the Horn of Africa. On the one hand, there must be joy and relief at their new freedom after months of confinement following their Empire's collapse in defeat; and, on the other hand, a return to an Italy still at war, in partnership with Germany and Japan against the Allies. To many of them it must have seemed that they were jumping out of the frying-pan and into the fire. Would they be treated as heroes on their homecoming – or as unwanted refugees who must be housed and fed, another burden on a hard-pressed State?

That the best-laid plans can and do go wrong I discovered as soon as the first convoy was halted. In building our camp I had ordered that a hessian-screened 'smoke-cho' be dug 50 yards downwind from the tents. In the absence of seats the askaris positioned themselves on to a pole stretched across the long slit-trench from which smoke billowed whenever the lid was lifted. This was fine for troops, who neither wanted nor expected anything more elaborate. What I had not considered was the provision of latrines for the use of the internees when their convoys were halted at the block. It had not occurred to me that after a mere 20-mile journey, with only another 20 to go, the call of nature would be so insistent. No sooner had the first four trucks in a convoy been called forward than one woman after another jumped down in search of a latrine only to find none available. Had I allowed them to go off to the askaris' cho they would have formed long queues which would delay the convoy and throw the pre-embarkation process timetable out of gear, and I would lose control of the essential passport and documentation examination. I decided to let matters take their course. Those women who could not hold out simply had to squat down beside the road and for a few moments throw aside their natural modesty. As soon as the last convoy of the day had been cleared the troops went to work shovelling sand in order to prevent disease being carried by swarms of flies attracted to the scene as iron filings to a magnet.

Working my way one morning from the back to the front of a 3-ton truck two weeks into the repatriation I found myself face-to-face with an escaping prisoner-of-war unconvincingly disguised as a woman. Her jet-black hair was cropped short and her features, thin and bony, were those of a man without any softening femininity. She seemed to have no bosom beneath her shirt-blouse and a faded, yellow divided skirt added to her masculine appearance. Her answers to my questions came in a low, uncertain voice. I drew my revolver and in French ordered, 'Come with me. I believe you are an escaping prisoner-of-war.' Without any further word, and to total silence from the other women, she rose to her feet, climbed over the tailgate and jumped to the ground. Calling a sentry as escort I took her to my tent. Now I suddenly realised I was in a predicament. What should I do next? Perhaps seeing my indecision she began to protest that she was a woman. I looked closely at her. Everything about her pointed to her being a man: sallow skin, no makeup, the short hair and the clothes, even men's sandals. All in all, I thought, a pretty poor disguise.

I broke the silence that had fallen between us. 'You will wait here until the Military Police come from Berbera', I told her, anxious to get the convoy moving again. Looking me in the eye she slowly undid her shirt buttons and pulled the shirt open to reveal her chest. It was as flat as a board, with a few short, black hairs in the centre and small nipples that might just as well be a man's and my expression told her so. Without a word she unbuckled her leather belt and lowered her divided skirt. What happened next seemed to go into slow motion. With a hand on each hip she pushes down white, cellular pants to her knees. I see a thick, black, black triangle. Nothing else is there! I stare in disbelief. She must be a man, she has to be a man! I bend down and peer to see if in some extraordinary fashion a man's genitals had been taped out of sight. No, there are none. With two older sisters I was well enough aware of the differences between the sexes – they had shown an intense, precocious curiosity in discovering that difference when we were young – and now I have to force myself to admit that I have made a serious mistake. I ask her to accept my apology. With a curt nod she gives me the impression that she understands my dilemma. Is this just wishful thinking on my part? Am I clutching at straws? I leave the tent and stand outside to allow her to dress herself.

It is possible that the incident might have passed away unnoticed, that she was not disposed to make an issue of it, but when Lapthorn laughed as I escorted her to the truck and his raucous laughter was taken up by the waiting women I had a grim foreboding of trouble. I did not have long to wait. Early the next morning, at about seven o'clock, a bright yellow staff car approached at speed from Berbera. It stopped at the roadblock and an officer wearing a Military Police armband climbed out. 'I am Captain Coulthurst', he announced. 'I am the Deputy Assistant Provost Marshal. An Italian woman has complained to the International Red Cross that she was stripped at this roadblock by a British officer. I have come to take from you a Summary of Evidence that may lead to your court-martial.' He said no more than I had steeled myself to expect. As we walked to my tent I saw myself cashiered and thrown out of the Army, only to be conscripted at once as a private soldier. Commissioned and cashiered in the space of six months! Could there possibly be a greater disgrace? The darkest moments in my entire service began before breakfast that day.

Coulthurst took a full statement from me, asking question after question as he tried to discover whether I was a fool or had a sexual motive for the incident. I could only pray that the simple truth would shine out to save me. If I had set out to strip a woman, would I have chosen as my victim a poor creature so strongly resembling a stunted man, I asked? Would not I have pretended that an attractive, well-formed young woman was a suspected prisoner-of-war in disguise? Had he seen and interviewed the unfortunate woman and, if he had, could he not understand my dilemma and the actions that followed? His only reply was to order me to answer his questions. Two hours later Coulthurst left for Berbera, warning that things looked very black indeed for me. At last I was alone with my misery, watching the dustcloud that flew up to trail the staff car bearing my fate in his black notebook. At just 19 I felt very, very lonely. How soon, I wondered, would I be relieved of my duties and placed under arrest pending a court-martial? It was not easy to carry on as though nothing had happened but it had to be done. Pride forbade me to discuss the matter with Sergeant Lapthorn and in any case I convinced myself, rightly or wrongly, that it was his coarse laughter which had provoked the complaint. Convoys came, were halted, documents were inspected and questions asked, convoys rolled off towards Berbera.

A fleeting cheerfulness returned when I climbed aboard yet another truck, to be greeted with blown kisses and cries of joy from the three girls of the famous picnic, the two Olgas and Gina. Their farewell waves continued until their truck rounded the hilly curve and disappeared from sight. My heart sank again into my boots. I found myself forever looking for the Provost Marshal's ghastly yellow car coming to haul me off under arrest, and wondered whether I ought not to write to my mother to warn her of my impending disgrace. It would not be easy to set down the full facts. Who would believe my explanation of the incident if the Army found me guilty of disgraceful conduct? The most loving mother's belief in her son's innocence must be strained to the limit in such circumstances. I decided not to write.

My next visitor was the battalion's second-in-command. Major Field had driven from Dire Dawa to interview me and report back to the commanding officer. He was stiffly formal as he listened to my account of the incident and, like Captain Coulthurst, cross-examined me so that every detail was brought out and noted. I was discovering for myself just how coldly the Army treats its transgressors – even before they are found guilty of any offence. Field had brought me no comfort, no promise to look for mitigating circumstances to advance in my favour. I realised that I was on my own in this affair.

On 18 May, when the block had been established for three weeks and scores of convoys had gone through, I boarded yet another motorcoach and made my way as usual to the back rows. Routine and anxiety had not blunted my sense of duty as I inspected documents and asked my questions again and again, looking each internee in the face as I did so. Two rows from the back sat a young woman of about 28, her face well made-up with cosmetics and lipstick, wearing a gaily-coloured summer print dress and a matching bandeau around her head. Beneath her dress shapely breasts swelled. She passed me her passport without a word as I stood before her. 'Nome del padre?' A pause before she answered in a low voice. 'Nome della madre?' Another low answer. There was no need for further questions. I drew my revolver. 'You are an escaping prisoner-of-war. Come with me.' A woman sitting in the row immediately behind began to scream hysterically, others joined in with shouts and abuse. In a moment the bus was in bedlam. 'Silenzio!' I roared, and as suddenly as it had begun the uproar ceased. Rising to her feet the young woman said, in a deep male voice, in English, 'It is the fortunes of war, Tenente'. This time there was no mistake. My prize was Lieutenant Alberto Russo of the Italian Colonial Infantry.

Taking him to my tent and posting a sentry outside I ordered the lieutenant to strip naked and searched every item of his women's clothing. He had paid great attention to detail, I discovered. He wore pink, lace-trimmed pants and padded brassiere, a matching set provided, he told me, by his girl-friend, and his summer dress was long to hide his masculine legs which, although shaven, could have given him away. The nail varnish on his fingers matched his lipstick and on his feet he wore sandals with fashionable, raised heels. A sketch map I found in his handbag detailed the route from Addis Ababa to Berbera and showed troop dispositions and the locations of the seven roadblocks. He had also a small compass. This was a well-planned escape attempt, beautifully executed. Now the lieutenant wanted to have nothing more to do with his women's clothing and asked for a shirt and a pair of trousers, which I was only too pleased to give him, seeing in his capture my possible salvation. Gratefully accepting my offer of four fingers of 'Old Angus' whisky – motto: 'Mild as a Lamb' – he told me his story in excellent English.

He had escaped from the PoW officers' compound in Addis Ababa as soon as he learned of the impending repatriation from Berbera and by some means or other managed to get into the women's compound where his girlfriend was interned. There she and the other women provided him with a false passport, complete with photograph of himself in disguise. He lived with them for eight weeks before the convoys began to form for their long journey to the port, and with their connivance evaded detection at every one of many inspections and rollcalls. His good fortune continued, with the women's help, at each transit camp on the road to Berbera. He passed undetected through six successive roadblocks until he reached mine, the last in Africa, a bare 20 miles from the ships that could carry him home to Italy. I offered my sincere congratulations – we were now on cordial terms and there was nothing to be gained by treating him other than with courtesy and some admiration – and asked him to autograph his brassiere for me as souvenir of our encounter. He signed it in ink: 'Alberto Russo, Lieutenant.' Defeated generals surrender their swords, recaptured lieutenants their brassieres.

In response to my call on the field telephone, South African military police arrived at the block to take the lieutenant to the cells at Berbera. For a moment I hoped he might get a glimpse of *Rex* and *Italia* before realising how painful this would be for him. So near and yet so far. He had almost made it – and in some ways I wished he had. That same evening a jubilant Captain Coulthurst drove up to the roadblock bearing a bottle of whisky to share with me. I was the hero of the hour. My capture of Lieutenant Russo had convinced the Army, and the International Red Cross, that there had been some justification for my earlier actions. All proceedings against me were now to be formally dropped and the incident put down to 'an excess of zeal on the part of a junior officer'. I owed a great deal to Lieutenant Russo and hoped that one day we might meet again.

The Snake Man

WITH MORE THAN FORTY OFFICERS at his disposal the colonel nonetheless decided that I was the one to send on two consecutive courses down in Kenya although as a recent arrival from England I was probably less in need of training than most. My orders were to attend the Junior Tactical Course at the Small Arms School at Gilgil and then go to Nakuru for the Physical Training Course. These would take me away from the battalion for eight weeks, including a week's journey-time each way. I had not lost my determination to get to the Middle East but a new obstacle now lay squarely in my path: I had quickly learned to speak Swahili well enough to pass the written and oral examination and was now more valuable to the KAR, who would be even less willing than before to let me go. I decided that whilst I was in Kenya I would arrange a few days' leave to be spent in lobbying the patient but hitherto unyielding Military Secretary at Command Headquarters.

All officers and British NCOs were required to pass the Swahili examination within six months of joining the KAR; it was clearly more sensible for a relatively small number of Europeans to speak the lingua franca than it was to attempt to teach hundreds of thousands of African soldiers, from countless tribes and sub-tribes, to speak English. Platoon commanders were, of course, ideally placed to learn Swahili for the platoon is a small unit of thirty or so men and their leader must come quickly to know each man individually – not just his name and his degree of soldierly proficiency but also his tribe, his personal qualities, his temperament, strengths and weaknesses. None of this would be possible without a sound working knowledge of Swahili.

Both on and off duty it was the task of the officers of 'D'

Company to weld together into a fighting unit men of a dozen tribes, from southern Tanganyika, where it bordered Nyasaland, to the north of the country; and from Lake Victoria in the west to Dar es Salaam on the Indian Ocean. Visiting 16 Platoon's Lines in the early evenings I soon found myself able to hold simple conversations with the askaris so that it was not long before I could listen to, and understand, their family troubles back home, troubles which they ingenuously assured me could only be sorted out by the granting of compassionate leave. More often than not news from home, written by the village's professional letter-writer, told them that their cattle had been stolen or their house had fallen down, or their wife had run off with another man. Censoring mail also helped to improve my vocabulary and grammar as it was necessary frequently to refer to the dictionary and 'Steere', the Swahili textbook which was our bible. Swahili spoken well is a delight to the ear and Tanganyika Swahili is regarded as truly *safi*, really clean. I enjoyed the process of learning; for some strange reason the elegant subjunctive mood held a special appeal for me.

I was determined to turn my platoon into a proficient, self-contained, and self-reliant little force as long as I stayed with the battalion. Already I was finding myself developing a strong affection for my askaris, together with a deepening sense of responsibility for their well-being, notwithstanding my most recent application to join a parachute unit now being formed in the Middle East for which volunteers were being sought.

I decided that Tomasi and I would spend the night with 'B' Company at Jijiga on our way through to Addis Ababa to join a convoy for Nairobi. This would give me an opportunity to see Frank Bissley again after six months and meet his company commander, Captain Ionides, who had been away hunting near Mount Chelalo in Abyssinia's Arussi country when Frank joined the company. Captain Constantine John Philip Ionides, or 'Iodine', as he was inevitably called, was the battalion's eccentric, a distinction he strove tirelessly to maintain. Indeed, he had gone to great pains to establish himself as a legend in eccentricity in the KAR's six peacetime battalions from the moment he joined the regiment in 1926. His had been a conventional early childhood in the bosom of his Greek family living in Hove, on the South Coast, until it was decided that he should go to Rugby, whose emphasis on athleticism and classical teaching seemed more appropriate for him than Winchester, his father's old school, or his mother's preference, Eton. That Rugby was both the setting for *Tom Brown's Schooldays* and the birthplace of what became known and revered as 'the Arnold tradition' throughout middle-class Britain were seen as further important considerations in its favour.

It would have spoiled Ionides' self-deprecatory stories had he admitted that his days at Rugby were happy, for his aim from the day he arrived at the school was to make a cult of his faults so that they might be seen as evidence of his virtues. He described his time at Rugby as hesitant and erratic, and his school reports as thoroughly disapproving. 'The worst boy I have ever had to teach' and 'He will have to leave at the end of term if there is no improvement' were probably the least bad of those he quoted. No matter what school custom might demand Ionides was sure to defy it for the sake of his growing reputation as 'odd man out'. The Rugby system of 'privileges', introduced by Dr Arnold, included fagging for older boys and, depending on seniority, of being allowed to put one hand in a trouser pocket in your second term, and both hands in the third term; the wearing of turnover collars to distinguish seniors from juniors; and so on. For his deliberate transgressions against the code Ionides claimed to have been beaten more and more frequently by the prefects upon whom the keeping of law and order was devolved. Ever bigger beatings were, of course, what he needed to promote that necessary personal conspicuity which set him apart from his fellows.

Notwithstanding his self-proclaimed state of continuous rebellion against authority he was at the same time developing the interest in natural history which was later to become his life's work. His frequent forays into the Warwickshire countryside were rewarded with grass snakes to be skinned, field mice for dissection, dead birds to be boiled down to their skeleton for study. To add spice to his growing reputation he put it about that he went poaching at night-time, setting rabbit snares and catching pheasants whilst eluding gamekeepers whom he kept in a state of infuriated bafflement. In all probability Ionides' three years at Rugby were no less happy and varied than those of most other boys, but there lay within him an irresistible urge for distinction which could most easily be achieved by 'showing off' and courting the thorough disapproval of the teaching establishment – who had doubtless seen many boys like him passing through their hands. Contrary to his boasts, by all accounts he left behind him no legend as a hell-raiser, only a reputation for having fun and being 'a bit of an exhibitionist'.

In Alan Wykes' book, *Snake Man*, Ionides claims that he was expelled from Rugby on suspicion of theft of another boy's money from a changing-room, a charge he refused to attempt to disprove because he was so thoroughly out of favour with the headmaster that it would be a waste of time to present evidence which would clear him. His account of his expulsion is unconvincing, and a little later in the book it emerges that it was because his work was so poor that his father was asked to withdraw him at the end of that current term. To 'admit' that he was expelled gave him the glamour he craved. It is not improbable that he may have found the circumstances of the famous, contemporaneous Archer-Shee theft case – young naval cadet against Their Lordships of the Admiralty – so appealing to his nature that he adapted elements of it for his own purposes.

Whereas other boys went matter-of-factly to crammers to prepare for the Army Entrance Examination for the Royal Military College, Sandhurst, Ionides claimed that he 'exhausted three crammers' before passing in 1920. That the Army accepted him as a Gentleman Cadet is proof that there was no cloud of dishonesty over his head but his talent for embroidering the most ordinary account made him, at least in his own eyes, more interesting and unusual than his contemporaries. It was no less typical of him than that he should make a point of stressing that he was nearly thrown out of Sandhurst, passing out third from the bottom. No sooner was he commissioned a second lieutenant in the 24th Regiment of Foot, the South Wales Borderers, than he set out to prove himself an impossible soldier and a worse officer.

Ionides joined his regiment's 2nd Battalion at Jhansi, in India's United Provinces in 1922 and soon, by dint of deliberate, systematic defiance of military discipline, isolated himself from his brother officers and antagonised his commanding officer. Not for him a smart, soldierly appearance. If he is to be believed, he would appear on parade wearing football boots or tennis shoes, giving as explanation that his regulation boots had a nail in them. His uniform was invariably creased and crumpled where it should have been fresh and well-starched; and he made a point of saluting without a hat – 'after all, saluting is only a habit one tends to get into'. Yet clearly there was more to Second Lieutenant Ionides – 'Greek', as he was then known – than a bloody-minded individualism and something of this began to emerge at the same time as he was developing great skill as a hunter. When his battalion moved to Cox's Bazar on the East Bengal coast Ionides took off on a solitary leave to shoot in Tenasserim and the Irrawaddy Delta in Lower Burma. Making his way down the Arakan Yoma – which in the Burma Campaign of 1942–5 was to see much bitter fighting between the KAR and the Japanese Army – he hunted tiger, buffalo, leopard, crocodile, and black buck with skill and courage that marked him as exceptional. There was, though, no place in the British Army for a junior officer bent on defying, even deriding, the system and mocking its traditions without making a contribution that would outweigh often childishly-selfish demonstrations of eccentricity. According to him, his application to transfer to the King's African Rifles was granted with unusual swiftness – and the South Wales Borderers heaved a collective sigh of relief at his departure.

The colonial infantry had always been less formal in many ways than the British Regular Army with its proud battle honours won over three centuries. The KAR had a way of life all its own, fostered since the regiment's creation on 1 January, 1902, just twenty-five years before Ionides joined the 6th Battalion at Dar es Salaam, when there was only a handful of Europeans in East Africa, men and women who had followed the few pioneers who trekked from the Coast in the 1880s. These settlers – colonists and frontiersmen in a great tradition – came to hew a living out of this unknown land and the KAR sprang naturally from the needs and the spirit of those earliest days of the British presence.

Ionides fell in love with Africa – he told me he knew it was his destiny to do so – and as quickly fell out of love with the Army so that in 1929 he resigned his commission to join Kenya's Game Department. The square peg had found a square hole at last. His recall to the KAR at the outbreak of the war in September 1939 provided him with opportunity to indulge in the maverick behaviour which had facilitated his removal from Rugby and the South Wales Borderers. This born 'irregular' was again expected to conform and the result was a foregone conclusion. Had the Army authorities just glanced at his Army Form 199A, chronicling every detail of his entire military service history, they would have left him where he was: his years as a Game Ranger had brought out his superb qualities as hunter and conservator but now they posted him to 3rd/6th KAR, where once again he would exploit every opportunity to be a disastrously bad soldier and selfish officer. Ionides' background was unknown to me when I drove into 'B' Company's camp at Jijiga late that afternoon and met him for the first time. It was not until years later, when Alan Wykes' book was published, that I began to understand him better and was able to make a little sense of my scant knowledge of him.

The company paraded for 'Retreat' a few minutes after my arrival and as a visitor I stood and watched a ceremony which, for me, never lost its impressive solemnity, especially when performed in a lonely desert outpost. But that day was different, horribly different. Captain Ionides strolled on to the parade ground wearing a creased khaki shirt and crumpled shorts, no stockings, and tennis shoes on his feet. He wore no hat, and his greying hair was thick and unkempt. To my amazement, Bissley, the only subaltern in camp, was dressed in the same fashion as he ambled on parade and languidly saluted his company commander as though it were all a frightful bore. It was easy to see that each was trying to outdo the other in a demonstration of contempt for military good order and discipline. As I watched this farce unfold my temper rose. 'B' Company's askaris deserved better than this from their officers. I could see at once that discipline was at a low ebb, that training had been long neglected. The troops mustered in untidy ranks without 'dressing to the right'; their ragged arms drill spoke volumes; and their untidy khaki uniforms were a disgrace to the regiment. It came as a relief when Ionides dismissed the parade and the askaris sauntered to the Lines for their evening meal.

Dinner in the company's mess that night was primitive, food so poor that no self-respecting mpishi would ever have allowed it to come from his kitchen. The chipped plates with vestigial blue rim, cracked mugs, and dull knives and forks told of the neglect and indifference that ran from top to bottom of 'B' Company. Only Ionides' tales of hunting the rare nyala, a mountain bush-buck, in Abyssinia redeemed the evening, making fascinating and instructive listening to one so new to Africa. Nobody would deny that Ionides had courage. Few men would have gone alone pre-war, as he had, on months' long big-game hunting in the Arakan, far from any help if things went wrong. He showed courage in another form on a visit to 'D' Company at Mandera: walking one afternoon in our kitchen garden, he disturbed a spitting cobra that shot its venom directly into his eyes. Very calmly he sat down in order to keep his heart-rate low and shouted for a bowl of milk to be brought at once so that he might wash out the venom. In his later life with snakes that same cool composure more than once saved his life.

Whatever I might have expected of Ionides, of whom I had heard a great deal, I found the change in Frank Bissley hard to believe. On board *Scythia* he had been sharp, intelligent, a keen officer and good company. Now, after six months with Ionides he had become slovenly, indifferent to the askaris in his refusal to have anything more to do with them than was absolutely unavoidable, and never speaking a word of Swahili. In a sense, I supposed, he had 'gone bush'. He sought constantly to justify himself by relating to anyone who would listen the latest twists and turns of his unceasing efforts to be transferred to a British regiment. Before leaving early the next morning for Dire Dawa and Addis Ababa I had a last, unavailing word with him. He repeated his conviction that only by continuing to behave in this fashion could he hope that the KAR would eventually grant his transfer, that his case would be lost if he admitted to understanding so much as a word of Swahili. I gave him up as a lost cause. Two years later he achieved the longed-for transfer and returned to his parent regiment, then fighting in Burma. Within days he was dead, killed in action at the head of his men in an attack against Japanese positions.

Ionides, too, won his battle with the authorities. He had petitioned for release from the Army from the moment of his recall. At 41 he was old for an infantryman in a first-line battalion and in 1944 was allowed to return to his life as a Game Ranger, leaving his successors to attempt to repair the damage he left behind him. I was glad to see him go. I had enjoyed his company and learned much of Africa from him but he had failed to honour his profession as a soldier and, even worse, he had failed in his duty to his askaris. After the war Ionides became a distinguished hunter before he transferred his interest from game and earned renown as an outstanding field naturalist and world authority on reptiles. Alan Wykes' adulatory biography significantly contains barely a word of Ionides' wartime service with the KAR. All in all, it was better for his reputation that a veil should be drawn over his inglorious military career.

The Faithful Servant

Tomasi and I were looking forward to our safari south. With any luck both of us would go on leave for a week or so after I had attended training courses at Nakuru and Gilgil in Kenya's White Highlands. To make up for his long absence Tomasi wanted to return to his village near Kisumu to see his father and mother and a girl named Serafina and needed at least seven days to do so. For my part I would stay at the Officers' Club in the centre of Nairobi, within walking distance of the Military Secretary who might grant me a transfer to Middle East Command.

A convoy of 15-cwt trucks due for major overhaul was assembled at Addis Ababa for the thousand-mile journey that would reverse the route that had brought us here six months earlier. The convoy commander read out standing orders on discipline and security, and issued Duty Officer and sentry rosters for overnight halts. Personal weapons and ammunition were checked and inspected for defence against bands of shifta who might launch an attack on us from the cover of the thick forests the convoy must pass through; and the last-but-one vehicle would carry a vigilant lookout man to keep the 'Arse-End Charlie' truck in sight at all times in case it broke down and was unintentionally left behind. Each European was allotted a vehicle he was to drive, accompanied by his personal servant or orderly and men going on leave. The trucks were loaded with 44-gallon drums of petrol, debes of oil and water, spare parts, personal baggage and bedding rolls, rations and cases of beer. Canvas chagouls were hung on the outside of each truck where evaporation would keep drinking water cool. We would make an afternoon start so that the first 20 miles could be treated as a last opportunity to detect and repair mechanical failures that came to light. The following day should see us setting out on our safari that might take two weeks or more in the heavy rains which were now falling almost without respite.

The dirt road was no more than a worn, muddy track with deep ruts and potholes and so slippery that ascending and descending the steep hills outside Addis brought speeds down to a snail's pace. Almost immediately my truck developed petrol-pump trouble and took its turn for repair with others that had fallen by the wayside. The omens were not good. All the vehicles were in poor mechanical state – they had covered huge mileages during the recent Abyssinian Campaign and were thoroughly clapped-out – and it was three days before we reached Moggio, not much more than 100 miles from Addis. Back in February, in the dry season, that distance was covered in five hours.

On Thursday, 23 July I ran over Tomasi. In teeming rain we were now approaching Neghelli, a small town 200 miles north of the border with Kenya's Northern Frontier District (NFD). As the truck passed over a deep hole in the road it lurched violently and a canvas bucket hanging on a rifle-clip in the cab and containing my whisky bottles flew out of the passenger side. Before I could put my foot on the brake pedal Tomasi had leapt from the truck and disappeared from sight. Until I stopped and climbed out I had no idea that anything was wrong. Then I saw Tomasi was lying motionless in the road, the truck's rear wheel having passed over the back of his right knee, grinding it into the stony mud so that bone and gristle were exposed in a bloody mess. The convoy halted and an urgent discussion began as Tomasi, barely conscious, was carried to my truck and laid on bedding in the back. He was clearly in intense pain and must be got to hospital with a minimum of delay. There was, though, no hospital conveniently just around the corner in the wilds of Abyssinia.

It seemed folly to turn around and head back to Addis Ababa. We had already taken seven days to get this far and with the rains falling ever more heavily the journey could take as much as ten days. Moreover, the truck was mechanically suspect and had several times demonstrated its unreliability. It would be all too easy to get stranded miles from anywhere – and there were also the shifta to worry about. Now that I had six months' experience in these parts I knew more about the marauding Somali shifta bands who roamed southern Abyssinia and the northern areas of the NFD armed with captured and discarded Italian Type 91 model rifles, pillarbox-red grenades, 9 mm Beretta pistols and submachine guns, and festooned with bandoliers. These were ruthless outlaws who killed for the sake of killing, holding human life cheap if it stood in the way of rape and pillage. A lone vehicle would stand no chance against them and a small askari escort would be no match for fifty, perhaps as many as a hundred, blood-thirsty bandits, hence the need for the system of well-disciplined, well-armed convoys of vehicles closed-up on one another for greater safety.

It was shifta custom to hand their prisoners over to the women to deal with, and we knew better than to allow ourselves to be captured. By all accounts the 'least worst' damage these shock-headed harpies inflicted on their victim was first to tie him to a tree, then rip open his belly with a razor-sharp dagger so that his intestines fell in a heap at his feet. Progressive, unspeakable mutilation might follow at their whim until death came at last, hours later. The convoy commander agreed that I had no alternative but to leave with a second truck as armed escort and fall-back in the event of breakdown and drive south as fast as the road allowed in search of a field hospital, or at least a medical officer stationed at an Army outpost. My fear was that with so much dirt lying deep in Tomasi's wound septicaemia or even gangrene would quickly set in. I was worried, too, that as a personal servant, not an enlisted askari, he might not have received any anti-tetanus protection. Meanwhile, I could only give him morphine injections. With another officer, a Lieutenant Collins, I set off with the two trucks and six askaris at first light the next morning. We found no medical facility at Neghelli but had not expected to do so and pushed on as fast as the terrain allowed to Mega, on the summit of the

Abyssinian escarpment overlooking the ochre-red floor of the NFD's desert wastes. Here we were faced with a difficult choice: two roads led out of Mega, one to the south-west towards distant Marsabit and beyond to Kenya's Central Highlands, the other to the south-east, to Moyale, 80 miles away, with Wajir 150 miles further on. Moyale and Wajir had been important KAR outposts before the war; now, following the campaign, they were supply concentration points but both were remote specks in a vast nowhere, and if neither had a medical officer I might have made a fatally-wrong decision in opting for them. It would have to be the Marsabit road.

No matter how carefully I drove over the atrocious track, doing all that I could to avoid the worst of the sickening bumps and deep holes, I knew that Tomasi was being thrown continually from side to side with every lurch as he lay on a makeshift bed in the back of the open truck. I was thankful that I could not hear the groans that I knew must escape him. We crawled down the precipitous escarpment with its seemingly endless succession of hairpin bends, leaving behind the lush grass waving in the cool, refreshing breezes of the high plateau and plunged into the furnace-heat of the desert that lay between us and Kenya's green farmlands. Tomasi's face had turned grey, a bad sign, and he could speak only with difficulty as he strove to hide his pain. We pressed on, rolling from side to side, smashing down on the springs, sometimes speeding up to skim over wavy, transverse corrugations that could best be taken fast, only to slow again to a bare walking pace. The torture went on hour after hour, the cab a fiery-hot oven even with the windscreen latched flat to catch an occasional rush of air. In this stifling wilderness I lost all track of time; nothing mattered, only to drive and keep driving until dusk.

Sweating and straining at the wheel I shared every moment of Tomasi's agony until such fatigue and black depression overwhelmed me that made it difficult to continue. I guessed that my blood sugar level had run dangerously low, and craved something, anything, that was sweet. Inspiration! Taking a tin of Nestle's condensed milk from my 'chop box' I punched two holes in the top and sucked and sucked as I drove until it was empty. The 'energy charge' revived me and gradually the overpowering sense of despair lifted. I made a mental note to remember the restorative powers of sweet, thick milk. Collins followed, sensibly keeping a mile to the rear to avoid the dense dustcloud we were throwing up. Once an hour we stopped to check on Tomasi's condition and give him water. He was still bearing up stoically, even managing an occasional weak smile as I assured him that it would not be long now before he was in a clean, cool hospital bed. This was no time to admire the giraffe loftily grazing the tops of thorn trees, or the ostrich and camels that kept pace alongside for a while before turning away into the scorched grey scrub, nor the gazelle that raced springing across the face of the desert. Absolute concentration was demanded if the next and the next and the next vicious rock or hole was to be avoided or at least minimised.

These were the tribal territories of the Arussi, the Galla, and the Boran, of the Degodiya, Turkana, the Rendille and the Samburu but there was never a settlement to be seen from the road. Occasionally, perhaps once in 30 miles, a lone figure would come into sight, standing stock-still close to the track leaning on his herd-stick, long spear in hand, naked except for a cloak of calf-skin thrown over one shoulder, his plaited hair heavily-greased and ochre-red, as he watched us approach then vanish in the dust-trail, trespassers on the land his people had roamed since time began.

We were now making our painful way through a kind of no man's land of endless horizons to Marsabit and had many hours' driving still ahead of us. The NFD extends from Lake Rudolf – now Lake Turkana – to the Somali border and consists of about a hundred thousand square miles of acacia scrub, laval desert, and broad areas of sand desert, almost twice the size of England. Termites' towers, like crude sculptures, in their hundreds grow tall from the baked earth and the only trees are the shadeless thorn trees. In the very heart of this flat land mass rises the volcanic outcrop that is Marsabit, with its mountains and forests, plantations and maize fields. A District

Commissioner was stationed in this Elysium and I hoped against hope that there might also be a medical officer there. We pulled up at last outside the DC's house. The Union Jack flapped lazily from a flagpole in his garden. There was no doctor here, he told us, and no Aid Post. We must push on. Exhausted and stiff and aching all over from being thrown about by the lurching and rolling, we climbed into the trucks for another long haul, first to Archer's Post, then to Isiolo, the northern approach to a richly-green, fertile Kenya.

Thirty miles from Marsabit the offside front tyre of my truck began to strip, throwing off chunks of rubber before we subsided onto the rim and came to a halt. We would spend the night here, we decided, and make repairs while the evening meal was being cooked. A major problem emerged: already I had had two unrepairable punctures and a blow-out and was now out of spares. The other truck was no better off. We debated whether to cannibalise Collins' truck so that I could drive on alone until I remembered that we had passed an overturned, abandoned 3-tonner 20 miles back. With any luck we might salvage its wheels: even though they would be of bigger diameter than those of my 15-cwt they might fit to its hub-studs. Leaving one truck and two armed askaris with Tomasi, Collins and I went back along the road with jacks, wrenches, tyre-levers, and spanners – and four burly soldiers whose strength would be needed to manhandle the 3-tonner. We could only hope that at least two of its tyres were sound.

It was not until the early hours that we returned with a pair of wheels and fitted them in readiness for a start at first light. Despite our weariness spirits rose now that we were on the final lap; if only the trucks would keep going Tomasi should be in hospital late that afternoon. Out of the desert at last, and on to the luxurious, unimaginably-smooth metalled road that led into the White Highlands, we raced for Nanyuki. By four o'clock Tomasi was in the clean, cool bed I had promised him, sedated and free at last from the pain he had endured so bravely, and waiting to be wheeled to the operating theatre. I visited the hospital the next morning. Tomasi was set to make a full recovery, the doctor assured me, although it would take some weeks before he would be able to walk again. Driving out of Nanyuki on the Nairobi road I wondered whether we would ever meet again. I hoped so. But in any case, I told myself, perhaps I had repaid a little of the debt I owed him for his selfless care in nursing me through dysentery.

As soon as I had attended the courses at Nakuru and Gilgil, I hitched a lift to Nairobi in an RAF Anson aircraft and at once made an appointment to see the Military Secretary. I had decided to drop my request to be transferred to a British regiment in the Middle East; instead I would seek his confirmation of the strong rumour that an East African brigade was shortly to embark for Ceylon to begin jungle training prior to being sent to Burma. I reasoned, rightly as it turned out, that a Military Secretary must look favourably on a young officer keen to see some fighting and would agree to the domestic transfer I had in mind.

My posting to 11 (Kenya) Battalion of the KAR proved to be an unmitigated disaster, once again underlining the sound common sense of that Army dictum, 'Never volunteer for anything'. From the moment of reporting at Yatta Camp on 26 October 1942, first to the adjutant, a long-faced Scot, and then to a gloomily-forbidding, taciturn Scottish commanding officer, instinct told me that I would not be happy here. To my astonishment I found I was to command a half-company of sixty recently recruited askaris, not a platoon as I had expected. This, I was told, would be a temporary measure as more platoon commanders would be arriving shortly. I soon found that the other companies already had three officers each, whereas my only assistant was a British Company Sergeant-Major. I faced up to a difficult task.

My 'official' 21st birthday came along at Yatta. In truth it was my 20th, and I could not bring myself to celebrate even a white lie birthday so I ignored it. I had joined up under age, adding exactly one year in the interests of being able to remember if challenged. Back in June 1940 I had enlisted in the Royal Marines but had been thrown out a week later when I failed to report for duty with my birth certificate as ordered. After a brief pause in which to plan my next move I enlisted as a private in The Buffs, explaining that I was born in Australia and could not obtain my birth certificate. Nobody pressed the point. I often wondered what sort of war I would have had as a marine.

There was no lack of inspections in 11 KAR. We seemed to be for ever laying out kit and inspecting it in the Lines, and laying out arms and equipment on company parade grounds for somebody else's inspection. The Commanding Officer's Inspection scooped-up all the other kinds and was a prelude to the Brigadier's Inspection which would shortly take place. Brigadier Stockwell had made a name for himself in the Abyssinian Campaign and was now expecting to lead 25 (East African) Brigade first in Ceylon and then in Burma. His Inspection, announced with two or three days' warning, was preceded by intense, unceasing activity throughout the battalion. Platoon, company and battalion drill parades rehearsed every conceivable movement in the Drill Book; stones were whitewashed at the camp's entrance gates; and weapons were stripped, cleaned and oiled again and again. Finally, every item of equipment inventoried on Army Form G1098 was laid out, stood up or driven on to the parade ground. Latrines, cookhouses, and stores were brought to perfection in the way only the Army knows.

The British Company Sergeant-Major and I had no rest or sleep the night before the Inspection, spending long hours fitting the askaris properly into their uniform and equipment; tugging, loosening, tightening and fastening webbing belts; checking that haversacks contained exactly the correct items, properly packed; waterbottles filled; and each man's fifty rounds of ammunition accurately counted. Repeating these procedures sixty times was a monumental task. At 6 a.m. I held a final rifle inspection to catch any specks of dust before dashing off for a quick sluice of the face and changing into clean uniform before returning to my nannying and the commanding officer's final rehearsal.

The battalion forms up with 'A' Company on the right, then 'B' and 'C', with 'D' Company – mine – on the left. Platoon commanders stand in front of their men, company commanders five paces in front of their officers. The adjutant takes over command from the British Regimental Sergeant-Major and brings the battalion to 'Attention' as the commanding officer marches forward. The staff car arrives, the brigadier steps out. Salutes are exchanged, the adjutant gives the command 'General Salute – Present Arms!' and the sound of bugles is momentarily drowned as the palms of 1,000 hands crash on to rifle-slings and 1,000 right heels thud to the sunbaked ground. The brigadier slowly inspects each company, each platoon, in turn. Laid out to the rear of each company is its Inventory of Equipment, its G1098, buffed, polished, oiled, green-blancoed, freshly-painted where appropriate. Trucks, Bren-gun carriers, 3-inch mortars, pioneer tools – picks, shovels and the like – sparkle or gleam where they should sparkle or gleam.

At last it is the turn of 'D' Company. Up and down the ranks walks the brigadier, escorted by the commanding officer, the adjutant, the British Regimental Sergeant-Major and the African Regimental Sergeant-Major – and me. Then to the G1098. Standing beside him I wait to be dismissed. He speaks. 'The company is very good. But you – you haven't shaved.' I saluted. He turned away. The brigadier was observant. I had not shaved that morning, but at eight o'clock the night before so that nothing should interfere with my efforts to get the askaris fully ready for his Inspection. Little more than twelve hours' growth had done for me. My anger and frustration, built up over weeks since I joined the battalion, boiled over. As soon as the parade was dismissed I marched into the adjutant's office and asked for an interview with the commanding officer.

Colonel Church sat in his chair, staring at me without a word, his face black as thunder. He had heard the brigadier's rebuke. 'Sir, I wish to be transferred to another battalion. It is impossible to be efficient in this battalion when I command two platoons and have only a CSM to assist me. Other companies have at least four officers. I have been up all night getting the askaris ready and shaved last night to save time this morning.'

'I will not transfer you', said Colonel Church, raising his voice. 'You will stay here, in this battalion.' I would not accept this. 'I would prefer to be in the East African Military Labour Service than remain in this battalion', I replied angrily. That I would rather be navvying and road-building than stay in his first-line battalion enraged him still further. I didn't care.

'You – will – not – be – transferred! You will stay here. That is all. Dismiss!' I saluted and marched out. Three weeks later I found myself at brigade headquarters on a temporary posting as Brigade Orderly Officer, a junior staff appointment, whether I liked it or not. At least, I congratulated myself, I had escaped from 11 KAR and would never be sent back. Colonel Church and I did not meet again. He was posted elsewhere quite soon afterwards; and I heard that his wife left him for a duke.

What with attending the courses and being granted my transfer I had not replaced Tomasi but was employing an orderly selected from the company. Now that I was at brigade headquarters I must look around for a personal servant, I decided. It was then that I developed an eye infection, probably brought about by insects or dust, and was sent to a military hospital in Nairobi. My companion in the ambulance was another officer, Lieutenant Crawford, also with eye trouble but of a very different kind. He had enjoyed a serious drinking session in the mess the previous evening and when he looked at himself in the mirror the next morning he saw, with some difficulty and to his horror, that his eyes were fully crossed. Frightened out of his life, he spent an unavailing hour alternately shutting and opening his eyes in the hope that suddenly he would be able to see straight again, with each eye in its correct position. Now he was on his way to find out what a specialist might have in store for him.

My treatment was so painful that for several hours each day I could not open my eyes. There were no window-blinds in the

Personal Servant Tomasi Kitinya, son of Liech. Moshi, Tanganyika, April 1943

ward and the piercing clarity of the air at Nairobi's 5,600-feet altitude above sea level was more than I could bear. Nor were there any dark glasses to be had in the hospital, I learned, a deficiency which made me virtually blind each day until dusk. Lying in bed one afternoon, eyes closed, I heard a cheerful voice beside me. 'Jambo, Bwana', said Tomasi.

It was little short of a miracle that he had found me. Six weeks after his admission to hospital he was discharged as fit and at once made his way to Gilgil, where he knew I was to attend the first of the two courses. He was too late: I had gone on to Nakuru for the Physical Training Course. By one means and another he followed me there, to be told that I had returned to the battalion up in Somaliland. In fact, I was still in Nakuru, in hospital with badly-sprained ankles.

A well-known sportsman, Geoff Dyson, who after the war was to make a considerable name for himself as the father of British athletics' track and field training, had been sent out from England to run a programme of physical training courses aimed at toughening up the KAR. This was to be his first course since arriving in East Africa and was said to be based on commando training. Thirty of us were Dyson's guinea-pigs. A pair of ramped 'gallows' 15 feet high had been erected as the final hazard on an otherwise unexceptional obstacle course. At twenty-second intervals students were sent off in pairs to compete with one another in finishing first to shouts of encouragement and execration from Dyson and his assistants. It was inevitable that broken bones and sprains must result from jumping from that height on to rock-hard ground and Nakuru hospital received successive batches of casualties until only half of the original number of officers survived the 'gallows'. Another of Dyson's bright ideas had already led to losses: for some incomprehensible reason we were ordered to leap off the backs of trucks travelling at 15 miles an hour. I counted myself lucky that I had escaped with minor injuries that put me into hospital for three days, and it was during those three days that Tomasi arrived at the school and was told that I had left for Abyssinia and Somaliland.

Hitching a lift on a northbound convoy which he found halted at Nanyuki, he arrivedweeks later at Mandera, only to find that I had been transferred to another battalion, number and location unknown. He began at once to retrace his steps, staying a few days at each of the battalion's companies at Jijiga, Hargeisa, and Dire Dawa before arriving at Addis Ababa in the back of a truck driven by an Italian PoW 'trustie'. For two weeks he haunted the Army Service Corps depot, making himself useful in the hope of a ride on the next southbound convoy and explaining to the officers that he was Lieutenant Nunneley's personal servant with orders to rejoin him in Nairobi. In universal Army style he was made welcome by personal servants and orderlies wherever he found himself and never went hungry or lacked shelter during his travels.

Arrived back at last in Nairobi Tomasi found his way to the Officers' Club but drew a blank until quite by chance an officer who knew me heard him asking for me and told him I was at Yatta Camp with 11 KAR. It is no distance from Nairobi to Yatta and Tomasi hitched a ride without difficulty only to learn that I was in hospital in Nairobi. Back he hitched to Nairobi and at once made his way to the military hospital just outside the city. I listened to his story with amazement. Reliant on the goodwill and assistance of those whom he met on his odyssey Tomasi must have travelled almost three thousand miles in three months in his determination to rejoin me. I was as pleased to see him as he was to see me.

Of Human Frailty

THE LORETTO CONVENT requisitioned to serve as 25 (East African) Brigade Headquarters lay in the centre of Kurunegala, itself in the heart of Ceylon. The convent was a two-storey, colonial-style building, white-painted, whose wide frontage was set back from the road by a crescent-shaped driveway guarded by a small gatehouse. A long, cool cloister at the rear overlooked gardens bordered by tall trees from whose branches scores of flying foxes hung upside down until any sudden noise sent them wheeling in the sky for a few minutes before gliding back to their roosts.

It was no wish of mine to be attached to brigade headquarters. I was still paying the price many months later for angering the commanding officer with my impertinence in demanding a transfer from 11 KAR and now reluctantly held the appointment of Brigade Orderly Officer, a sort of aide-de-camp to the Brigade Commander. My other duties included commanding the Defence Platoon and dogsbodying at every job beneath the notice of staff captains and their seniors. At long last, though, the end of my sentence was in sight: following months of repeated requests it had been agreed that I would be transferred back to 36 KAR* as soon as the battalion arrived from East Africa for jungle-warfare training. I couldn't wait for my day of release.

Early one August afternoon shortly after our arrival in Ceylon, when senior staff officers had gone off to explore the surrounding countryside for suitable training areas, I was Duty Officer when a shouting mob of a hundred or so angry, bare-headed, African soldiers thronged to the convent gates

---

* On 1 June 1943 a new system of nomenclature was brought into operation. In general this system was applied by abolishing the oblique stroke used to separate the battalion from that of the regiment and adding letters to indicate the territory where the battalion was recruited. Thus 3rd/6th KAR became 36 (TT) KAR.

demanding to see the Bwana Mkubwa, the Big Boss, otherwise the brigadier. I went to investigate and turned out the Guard. A mob must have a ringleader. That day it was a Kikuyu corporal from Brigade Signals who pushed his way to the front and faced me. I demanded to know why they were here, what the shauri was about. The men's complaint poured from his lips in an angry torrent: on arrival in Ceylon all African troops had been ordered to shave their heads as a hygiene measure. That, the corporal told me, shouting to make himself heard over the racket going on around us, was all very well for ordinary askaris, who anyway shaved their heads in accordance with KAR custom, but signallers were superior to infantry askaris and should not be required to shave their heads.

This was plainly an issue beyond the authority and capability of a lieutenant to attempt to deal with and I ordered the shouting crowd to disperse and return at once to their Lines, with the promise that their complaint would be reported to the brigadier. The signallers were far too worked up to obey. They must have held a big baraza which had culminated in their decision to demonstrate, and as far as they were concerned military discipline was right out of the window for the time being. There was nothing for it but to arrest the corporal and I ordered the Guard commander to seize him and put him in the guardroom. At this, the pandemonium increased and a mass of soldiers pressed around me, demanding that I arrest them also. I picked half-a-dozen of them on a random 'you, you, and you' basis and as soon as the guardroom cell-door had clanged shut on these martyrs to the 'Cause of the Shaven Heads', the others at once quietened down and began to drift away. I had not been jostled or threatened in any way, the men had simply made their point noisily and in the most effective way they knew.

That the Kikuyu possessed a remarkable aptitude for Army signalling work and other technical specialist trades was undeniable, but that did not lift them above trained infantrymen. Discipline was restored when it was fully explained by the medical officer that the order was a health measure against the deadly scrub typhus they would be exposed to in Burma, and had nothing to do with inferiority or superiority. With the benefit of a crystal ball one might have seen in this incident the germinating seeds of Kenya's Mau Mau terror campaign which began in 1952 and led to the country's eventual independence eleven years later. Before the war the Kikuyu were not recruited into the KAR as, although they might in general be more intelligent and better educated than the 'martial' tribes such as the Kalenji and Kamba, they were notorious troublemakers.

Usually so equable in temperament the African soldier could surprise Europeans with outbursts of violence which brought tragic, usually fatal, consequences for those whose bad luck it was to find themselves in the wrong place at the wrong time. Incidents that in European eyes were of little significance could be of enormous importance to the African askari, sufficient to send him toppling over the brink to commit murder.

An urgent signal came in one morning from a battalion asking for a full medical team to be sent immediately to their jungle camp: an officer had been shot dead. A few minutes later came another signal: now three officers were dead, and shots were being fired inside the camp. A flow of messages brought more details as they became known: a company commander, a major, was holding his Company Orders when an African sergeant, brought before him on a disciplinary charge and awarded a punishment, broke away from his escort, seizing a rifle and ammunition as he did so, and fled into the nearby jungle. The alarm was raised and a platoon sent out to bring him back to face his punishment and answer further, more serious charges. The major was continuing with his 'Orders' when the sergeant crept up unseen to the open window and shot him dead at point-blank range as he sat in his chair. A second officer was shot and killed as he tried to escape from the office and then a third before the sergeant ran off again into the jungle. A hunt was now on, with orders to shoot to kill. There was no doubt that the crazed man would quickly be found. On training exercises in Abyssinia and British Somaliland I had watched askaris as trackers, marvelling at their skill as they picked up tiny signs: bent grassblades, disturbed pebbles, the faintest of footprints, even half of the rim-print of a boot heel or rubber-tyre sandal impressed in sand or soil. The sergeant was found, and died in a fusillade of shots. Later that day I went to the mortuary in Kurunegala where four shrouded bodies lay, three of them together, side by side, the fourth set apart on the far side of the room. Three lives taken in a few minutes of madness. And one summary execution.

Another officer was murdered at Kurunegala in April the following year. A detachment of the East African Military Police, manned by an officer and two British NCOs and a platoon of askaris was stationed in the town, now the headquarters of 21 (EA) Brigade recently arrived from East Africa for jungle training. One of the British NCOs had put an askari on a disciplinary charge and the officer awarded an appropriate punishment that nevertheless the askari considered unjust. Taking his rifle and five rounds of ammunition the soldier later crept up to the open window of the office-hut and shot the officer dead. In due course he was tried, found guilty, and shot by firing squad.

Lance-Corporal Kiption of my Defence Platoon, a Nandi tribesman, had been giving a good deal of trouble for several months. More than once in his service he had been reduced to private as punishment following charges concerned with good order and military discipline but had redeemed himself with good behaviour and zeal. Even so, I was far from happy with him and suspected that his violent mood swings could be due to his illegal smoking of bhang, hemp seed. In the past week or two I had several times admonished him for minor offences which did not warrant a formal charge and had noticed that his eyes were often wild and staring although each time he accepted my reprimand without a word of self-justification. By now we had moved to the ancient city of Anuradhapura where the headquarters operated from a large country house with a number of small bungalows set in the grounds as officers' sleeping quarters, usually on the scale of one per man.

Early one afternoon Kiption was reported missing from the Lines. There was a general shrugging of shoulders among the askaris and a resigned, 'That's mad Kiption all over. He'll be back when he comes to his senses.' When, however, Tomasi was warned by an askari that Kiption had been heard to threaten to kill me I sat up and took notice. It happened that a travelling field cashier was visiting headquarters that day and as I had room to spare in my bungalow I invited him to share it for the night. I thought it only fair to mention Kiption's threat, but although I stressed that I did not take it seriously, and was sure neither need he, I could see he was unconvinced. The night-time heat encouraged outdoor sleeping and Tomasi set out my camp bed on the narrow, open verandah as usual, the cashier's personal servant following suit. Announcing that I was a light sleeper who would wake at the slightest sound I suggested that, as a probably needless precaution, we should perhaps each sleep with a loaded revolver under our pillow.

I woke to find myself being shaken by an extremely agitated house-guest. After a night of fitful sleep, in dawn's early light he noticed a pile of neatly-folded clothes on the grass a few yards from the bungalow. A quick look told me that they were Kiption's; he must have decided to make me a present of them as much as to say, 'To hell with the Army! You can keep it – and my uniform'! Then we noticed tell-tale sandal prints in light dust beside my bed. Kiption had indeed paid me a visit, had stood beside me as I slept, probably armed with a rifle or a panga and with murder in mind – and must have decided at the last moment to spare me. Or was this, I wondered, his idea of a final warning? Who could know what was in a mind probably fuddled by bhang? Later that morning he was spotted sitting alone on the grass in the shadow of Anuradhapura's golden-domed dagoba and brought back under arrest wearing only his blanket, tribal-style. I made sure he was posted away as soon as he had completed 14 days' punishment and was once more a private. I acknowledged that it had been a close call, and if there were a next time my luck might run out.

My claim to be a light sleeper was a hollow one. I should have learned from an incident which occurred during the brigade's last night at Moshi, at the foot of Mount Kilimanjaro, before we moved to a transit camp outside Mombasa as a preliminary to embarkation for Ceylon. We were to make a dawn start for the road journey to Mariakani and the truck convoy was loaded up and made ready the day before. Reveille would sound at 5 a.m., when personal servants would bring their masters a mug of tea, and we would embus an hour later. Before I turned out the lamp in the tiny hut that served as my sleeping quarters I arranged my clothing and equipment in such a way that I could dress next morning in the dark, if need be. Tomasi would bring shaving water and tea, fold my bed and collapsible canvas basin-stand and roll them within my

valise, and we would be off and away within minutes. I laid my
.38 Smith & Wesson revolver and my watch with its brightly-
luminous hands on the bedside locker and went to sleep.
Revolver and watch were gone when Tomasi appeared next
morning. During the night a thief, probably a professional
from Moshi, not an askari, had crept into the hut and grabbed
the only easily-pocketable articles he could glimpse. I was in
serious trouble: the loss of a weapon is a court-martial offence.
It did not occur to me that I might have been stabbed with a
knife or hacked with a panga as I slept; that thought came
later. What worried me was that I would literally 'miss the
boat' if it were decided to court-martial me in Nairobi and I
decided to delay reporting the loss until the day before
embarkation.

Under open arrest, Sam Browne belt off and the charge
against me framed and read out to me so that I understood it, I
was marched in before Major-General Fowkes commanding
the division. The charge was again intoned. 'Do you wish to be
tried summarily by me or by court-martial?', he asked. 'By
you, Sir.' I was sure this would show him how keen I was to go
to Ceylon for jungle training, not to wallow in Kenya's luxury
life-style while waiting for military legal processes to take their
woefully long course.

'Do you plead Guilty or Not Guilty?'

'Guilty, Sir.'

'Have you anything to say in mitigation?'

'No, Sir.'

'I award you a Severe Reprimand and order you to pay for
the loss of the revolver. Dismissed.'

Months later, in the front line in Burma, I received a letter
from the Deputy Judge Advocate-General informing me that I
had been charged under the wrong section of the Army Act
and the proceedings would therefore be expunged from my
record. Would I, though, offer to pay the sum of six pounds six
shillings and eightpence, being the cost of the revolver? Yes, I
replied magnaminously, I would.

Trouble of a different kind came during a week-long jungle-training exercise in the north-east of the island, inland from Trincomalee, when yet again I was Duty Officer. It was late at night and I had just written the date, 11 December 1943, at the head of a letter to my mother when three rifle shots in quick succession rang out nearby. Almost at once a small crowd of villagers came running up the road in brilliant moonlight towards my tent – the only one with a hurricane lamp burning. I checked the time: 2240 hours. The headman panted that I must come at once: soldiers had shot their way into a house, murder was being done. I ordered the Guard Commander, Lance-Corporal Kiptanui, to come with me, rifle loaded. The village, named Horuwupotana, was a bare 200 yards away, set in a clearing ringed with thick jungle. Twenty or so single-storey, mud-block houses lay on each side of the road. Followed by the chattering, excited crowd the two of us ran to join the rest of the villagers staring from a little distance at the fourth house on the right-hand side of the road and listening to the screams coming from it.

I motioned Kiptanui forward and we began to walk slowly along the verge towards the house. Almost at once, though, I found he was hanging back until several yards separated us. Impatiently I gestured to him to close up on me but he made only a half-hearted move to do so and very cautiously I approached the house alone. As well as the screams I could now hear deep groans. My duty as a British officer was plain and simple: enter the house and arrest the soldiers. In these circumstances, easier said than done, especially as Kiptanui had come to a standstill 10 yards yards away and showed no inclination to come any closer. I did not relish the prospect of trying to arrest violent men who had shot their way into a house but I had committed myself to decisive action in the eyes of the villagers and must carry it out. I could not back off and send for reinforcements when every second counted. A curse on those inspiring adventure stories of Empire I had devoured so eagerly as a boy, in which British officers bravely did their duty, whatever the cost, or were handed a white feather by a beautiful girl with a contemptuous curl of her lip!

Creeping up to the house I stood beside the half-open, bullet-splintered door for a moment or two before kicking it wide and leaping inside and to the right to avoid being silhouetted in the moonlight. As I burst in three askaris threw themselves one after another through the open back window as though they were acrobatic tumblers and in seconds vanished into the black safety of the jungle. I was not sorry to have missed making their acquaintance. Immediately inside the door a man was lying on his side on the beaten-earth floor. By the light of the single oil-lamp I saw dark, arterial blood forming a lake around him as it flowed from a massive wound in his abdomen. I could not see then that his stomach had been blown away and his backbone shot to smithereens, but it was clear that there was no hope for him. Across the room, propped against the far wall, a young woman was quietly groaning, her bare left breast torn and bleeding from a raking knife-wound or richocetting bullet. Her sarong-like skirt had been pulled up high so that she was naked below the waist; it was plain that she had been raped, perhaps by one askari, perhaps by all three. There was nothing I could do for the man, and as I crouched beside him he gave a single, long sighing moan and died. I sent Kiptanui running for medical help and the woman was rushed by Army ambulance to hospital in Trincomalee. As far as my superficial visual examination could tell she had no other wounds.

A Criminal Investigation Department team from Colombo took statements and made plaster casts of the boot-prints found on soft ground outside the window. There was no doubt which battalion the askaris had come from – only one was in the immediate vicinity – and a ballistics man ordered that every one of a thousand or so rifles be examined to see whether any had been fired. There was little likelihood that the murderers would be caught: the odds against were far too great and within a day or two we would be on the move again. The detectives decided that the man had offered his woman to an askari earlier in the day, telling him to come to the house late that night. When three soldiers instead of one turned up he tried to send them away but they had taken a risk in leaving camp after 'Lights Out' and were determined to make it worthwhile. When he persisted in refusing to open the door they fired through it. At a range of two inches the bullets, deforming as they passed through the door, had done appalling injury to the man pushing against it. Two of the askaris had raped her before I burst into the house, the woman told the police. In the unusual circumstances of the incident I could find in King's Regulations no appropriate section under which Kiptanui might be charged for his failure and had to content myself with telling him he was a woman, not a worthy warrior of the great Nandi nation. Judging by his reaction my scorn cut him deeper than would have any formal Army punishment.

It was shortly after the murder at Horuwupotana that 36 KAR arrived in Ceylon and I was at last able to rejoin the battalion. By now I had been away almost a year and found there had been many changes, including a new commanding officer, but most of my former brother-officers were still there and I settled in at once with a sigh of relief. I could look forward to some serious training before we went off to fight the Japanese on the Burma Front.

Just as many askaris had never seen the sea until they embarked at Mombasa and marvelled at the ships which, they believed, must have long legs to enable them to stride across the sea-bed, so others had little experience of motor transport before they joined the Army. Those who had not learned to relate motion to speed sometimes paid a heavy price. Private Mumbwa was one of these unfortunates. It was not that Mumbwa was a founder-member of the Awkward Squad. Far from it. He was a good, conscientious askari, a heavily-built, coal-black Mgogo from Tanganyika's jungly savannahs, with that tribe's characteristic narrow, smiling eyes. More than once, though, he had lost his bush hat when it blew off his head as he rode in the back of an open truck and had been fined for careless loss. It had become something of a joke in the platoon to remind him, 'hold on to your hat'! As we embussed for a training exercise I laughingly reminded Mumbwa that if he lost his hat yet again he must expect big trouble from me. He shared in the jokiness. Ten miles along the road his hat blew off. Even before his mates could yell to the driver to stop Mumbwa had leaped over the tailgate and hit the road with his head at 30 miles an hour. He was deeply unconscious when we carried him to the truck and rushed him to hospital in Anuradhapura and remained in a coma until he died two days later as I stood at his bedside.

His body in a coffin bodged of rough planks, the funeral was in the town cemetery. I paraded his platoon and stood it to attention. Because Mumbwa was a pagan I could not use the formal burial service, with the solemn dignity of its words, and could only speak of the man and his qualities as soldier and comrade. My words seemed woefully inadequate and I wished I could have done better for him. The final, unforgettable poignancy came as the coffin was lowered and blood oozed from it on to one of the ropes. Each of us in turn saluted the good soldier Mumbwa before we marched off, back to our duties. In the fullness of time he would be reburied in a military cemetery with the respect he deserved.

Tension and a sense of urgency increased as the time approached for us to leave for Burma. The battles of Imphal and Kohima were raging as the Japanese fought to invade north-east India, and there were reports of heavy casualties on both sides. Rumour told us that our division was to fight throughout the south-west monsoon whose rains pour down from May to October. Overall the battalion appeared to be in good heart, well-trained and confident but to some, European and African, the prospect of fighting a fanatically-brave, merciless enemy at close quarters in the jungle filled them with dread. The sharp report of a single revolver shot rang through our jungle camp in the middle of a hot, humid afternoon. In the solitude of his hut Lieutenant Moore had put the muzzle in his mouth, pointed it upwards, and squeezed the trigger. He had joined the battalion only a week earlier and had appeared on parade hardly at all, reporting sick daily. He had probably suffered months-long, lonely hell of self-doubt with nobody, not even the padre, to whom he felt he could confide his fears. Within a day or two a replacement arrived from the reinforcement pool and Moore's name disappeared from the roll of officers and was quickly forgotten.

Shortly after Moore's suicide I visited a friend in another battalion, for sundowners. I found Lieutenant Thompson sitting in a safari chair outside his tent, a colourful backdrop of heraldic standards bearing his family's coat-of-arms hanging from the guyropes. Did he see himself as a knight waiting to joust on the Field of the Cloth of Gold, I joked? We chatted over a whisky about the forthcoming campaign, about the Japanese enemy, all the usual 'shop'. He spoke feelingly of his brother, a sub-lieutenant in HMS *Exeter*, who had been killed in the Battle of the River Plate when his gun turret took a direct hit from the German pocket-battleship, the *Graf Spee*.

Thompson was tall, strong, heavily-built. He exuded bonhomie and an enviable, absolute self-confidence. We had travelled out from England on the same draft and I enjoyed his company whenever we caught up with one another. He was, I knew, immensely proud of his parent regiment, the Gloucesters, with their two cap badges awarded to commemorate their most famous battle, when they were attacked from both front and rear simultaneously and their ranks stood back-to-back fighting off the enemy. For this they had earned the nickname 'The Fore-and-Aft'. He could recite the regiment's history back to its creation in 1694, he told me. In the middle of our last night in Ceylon he blew his brains out.

Wartime suicides and murders committed in the East African Forces were probably no greater proportionately than those in any army anywhere in the world. With hundreds of thousands of men under arms it was inevitable that crime and violence would occur to mirror peacetime life although the methods employed might sometimes be different. And only those who take their own lives can know, or think they know, their reason for doing so, for human frailty reveals itself in every condition of man.

A rumour had been circulating for several weeks that a

transport carrying East African troops from Mombasa to Colombo had been torpedoed in the Indian Ocean with heavy loss of life. A strict security blanket enveloped the incident but it was possible to piece together eye-witness accounts of the tragedy. The convoy that sailed from Kilindini in Mombasa's great natural anchorage on 6 February 1944 was a small one, just five transports escorted by a cruiser and two converted, former United States coastguard cutters. Earlier convoys of similar size had brought two-thirds of 11 (East African) Division to Ceylon for intensive jungle training and we were awaiting the remaining three infantry battalions and a complete artillery regiment of 850 officers, NCOs, and men to bring the division to full strength in preparation for campaigning in Burma. It was in one of these small convoys which crisscrossed the Indian Ocean that the brigade headquarters, of which I the reluctant junior officer, sailed in June 1943 aboard the British & Indian Steamship Navigation Company's *City of Paris*, of 9,000 tons. Two of the four transports were the *Khedive Ismael*, and the *Varsova*. All these ships were of similar size and carried 1,500 troops in their messdecks. Protection was provided by a cruiser which normally held station at the head of the convoy while two or more destroyers roamed the seas around us. Fearing submarine attack a high level of alertness was maintained at all times.

With Italy's North-East African Empire conquered, Abyssinia handed back to Emperor Haile Selassie, and the British occupying Italian Somaliland, Italian submarines no longer hunted the Arabian Sea and the western Indian Ocean; now their target was the Allied convoys passing through the Straits of Gibraltar to supply Malta and our armies in North Africa and southern Italy. Long-range German U-boats were at large in the Indian Ocean but these were used principally as the safest means of transporting precious materials needed for new secret weapons and munitions between Germany and Japan. The threat now was from the submarine flotillas of the Imperial Japanese Navy tasked to cross the Indian Ocean to attack Allied shipping.

The ships of the February 1944 convoy took up station as soon as they entered the open sea. In the forward port position was an elderly cruiser, HMS *Hawkins*, followed by *City of Paris*, the *Khedive Ismail* led the centre column, ahead of *Ekma*, and the starboard column had *Varsova* at the head, with *Ellenga* astern. Two 'P'-Class destroyers, *Paladin* and *Petard*, with Mediterranean combat experience, would take over from the coastguard cutters two days into the voyage. Three cable-lengths – 600 yards – separated the ships in both lineal and horizontal spacing.

Aboard *Khedive Ismail* there had been a pre-embarkation problem: how to accommodate a contingent of eighty-three servicewomen of Queen Alexandra's Military Nursing Service, the Women's Transport Service (First Aid Nursing Yeomanry) and the Women's Royal Naval Service in a ship with limited cabin accommodation? It was decided that all officers of 301 Field Regiment of East African Artillery below the rank of captain must transfer to *Ekma*. One of the junior officers thus deprived of his askaris and feminine company was Lieutenant Guy Yeoman, Gun Position Officer of a troop of 3.7 in. howitzers. Six days into the voyage the ships were approaching the Maldive Islands to the west of Ceylon. The early afternoon sun hung high in a cerulean sky and the dead calm sea was stirred only by creaming bow wave and white wake trailing towards the horizon. War was remote. It was the kind of day when those relaxing on deck after the mid-day meal would be agreeing with one another how infinitely preferable it was to travel hopefully than to arrive. Without warning the idyll aboard the *Khedive Ismail* was shattered by a tremendous, dull reverberating explosion amidships on the starboard side, followed immediately by dense clouds of dark smoke which enveloped the ship. Within seconds she was listing heavily to starboard, both bow and stern rearing high as the sea entered through massive rents in her hull.

There was no time to muster at boat stations, no time to attempt to lower lifeboats on the port side. Already the starboard-side lifeboats were under water. In the instant pitch-darkness, all electric power lost, those men and women in the cabins and mess-decks deep in the hull who had not died in the blast scrambled blindly on floors which were now walls and drowned as the sea rushed in. Two minutes later the *Khedive Ismail* began her plunge to the ocean-bed, leaving the few that had been on deck when the torpedo struck struggling towards wreckage strewn floating on the surface. *Ekma*, following close astern, her alarms ringing and all troops filing calmly up from below to muster on deck, immediately turned hard to starboard, heeling steeply; but even so she barely avoided sailing right through the scattered survivors and flotsam. On *Ekma*'s deck 301 Regiment's junior officers could only watch as their comrades perished.

The transports rapidly scattered, sounding their sirens as a signal to others each time they changed course, zig-zagging in an attempt to deceive the attacking submarine – there could have been more than one – and sailed on, leaving the destroyers which soon disappeared from sight. For the next three hours the troops 'Stood To' at their boat stations. (Those of us aboard the broken-down *Scythia*, off Dakar in December 1941, had experienced for three days and nights that same sense of loneliness, of waiting helplessly for a U-boat's torpedo to strike at any moment.) The submarine had infiltrated the convoy undetected from ahead and raised her periscope in the wake of the *Varsova* sailing parallel with *Khedive Ismail*, and fired a staggered fan of four torpedoes. The first two, from the forward tubes, registered almost-simultaneous hits on the *Khedive Ismail*. The other two torpedoes were fired from the bow starboard and bow port tubes, the first skipping the waves towards HMS *Hawkins* but passing safely beneath her bow, the second running under *Ekma*'s stern.

Paladin had sighted the submarine's periscope at the moment of firing and the two destroyers raced to try to pick up sounds on their anti-submarine detection indicator equipment. Very soon contact was made, followed by a furious pattern of depth charges from both destroyers. The remaining ships of the convoy were led away from the action by *Hawkins* firing starshells high into the sky as she departed. The depth charges forced the submarine I-27 – a giant, 2,000-ton 'I' Class of the Japanese Navy – to the surface where her crew strove desperately to bring her powerful 5.5-inch gun and triple machine-gun into action but were prevented by heavy Oerlikon quickfire from the destroyers. *Paladin* and *Petard* opened fire with 4-inch shells that proved ineffective despite numerous hits. (The reason? Incompetence by persons unknown. When the destroyers had last re-ammunitioned at Trincomalee Naval Base in Ceylon no armour-piercing shells were available, and the semi-armour-piercing shells which they had to accept proved useless at time of desperate need.)

In this extraordinary impasse – a disabled enemy submarine on the surface, impervious to the destroyers' gunfire, and the submarine's gun-crew being 'hosed-off' with *Petard*'s Oerlikon fire – *Paladin* hove-to and picked up those survivors who could be found. The destroyer captains then decided to torpedo I-27 but met with no success: the 'fish' went wide. Next, they tried dropping depth charges alongside her but these had only a slight effect and the submarine remained afloat, circling half-blind with one of her periscopes carried away. Forbidden by their military code even to contemplate surrender, the ultimate disgrace, I-27's crew could only wait for certain death by drowning or fire or blasting explosion, or a combination of all three.

Fresh perils faced the survivors aboard *Paladin*. Before they had time to change their sodden clothing the captain ordered through the loudspeakers, 'Get on deck at once and lie flat! About to ram submarine!' Packed like sardines in the narrow space outside the wardroom they waited for the impact of collision, which came minutes later with a great rending and grinding on the starboard side. At once all electric power failed, and oil and water began quickly to seep up towards the deck: the submarine's hydrofoil fin had torn a huge hole in *Paladin*'s side, flooding the engine and gear rooms. Scrambling to the upper deck, and preparing themselves for a second sinking, the survivors saw the submarine draw away and slowly submerge. Suddenly I-27 re-surfaced, leaping up in a cascade of water and spray, and charged towards *Paladin* lying dead in the water. In the nick of time a torpedo from *Petard* struck her and she blew up, throwing a huge column of water high in the air as she sank. One crewman was the sole survivor. Three hours had passed since the *Khedive Ismail* had gone to the bottom.

Most of *Paladin*'s crew and the survivors were transferred to *Petard*. HMS *Hawkins*, recalled to the scene, took *Paladin* in tow to beach her on Addu Atoll in the Maldives while the convoy, with only *Petard* as surface escort, proceeded under air cover to Colombo. Of the 1,511 on board *Khedive Ismail* when she sailed from Kilindini 30 out of 199 British officers survived; 113 askaris out of 787; 43 naval personnel out of 251; and 22 crew out of the ship's complement of 188. There were six survivors of the 83 servicewomen who had embarked: 2 WRNS out of 19; 3 QAIMNS out of 54; and one of the 10 Kenya Women's Transport Service. None of the three civilians on board escaped. Of all the eye-witness stories of the disaster, one remains to haunt: of a nurse who tried to scramble through her cabin porthole only to be trapped half-in, half-out, by her hips. Mercifully, her agony lasted only a few seconds before she was engulfed by the sea. She was the only nurse aboard whom I had known in Kenya.

Safely in Colombo, Guy Yeoman found his fears confirmed: 301 Field Regiment had been wiped out. Years spent training these pastoral African tribesmen in their gun-crew duties to achieve maximum accuracy had brought them to a high pitch of proficiency, fully ready to support their infantry comrades in attack and defence. Just nine of his troop's seventy-five askaris survived, among them fellow-tribesmen of 36 KAR's askaris – Wanyamwezi, Wasukuma, Yao, and Ngoni – who bore their ordeal with the utmost stoicism. Yeoman had no doubt that when the time came they would fight the Japanese in Burma with single-mindedness of purpose.

It is a legitimate dream of submarine commanders to sink the enemy's troop transports and thus aid their own land

N40605 Private Tomasi Kitinya (*right*) with Luo comrades.
Ceylon, June 1944

forces. With his single salvo the captain of the I-27 had come close to scoring a treble success: two fully-laden transports and a battle-cruiser, carrying all told some 5,000 fighting men. As it was, the loss of a complete regiment of artillery would seriously weaken the division's fighting capability. The tragedy of the sinking of the *Khedive Ismail* was compounded by the loss also of a complete unit of non-combatants, the matron and fifty-three nurses of the 11th Division's Base Hospital. All in all this action, which to those on board the transports was characterised by apparently-recurring sequences of order, counter-order, and disorder, may not have been fought in the highest traditions of the Royal Navy. In his book *The Second World War*, Volume v, Winston Churchill asks how it was that more survivors could not have been rescued.

★　★　★

It was a matter of days before the battalion was due to leave for Burma when an order came that personal servants must enlist as private soldiers and receive training as infantrymen or be repatriated to East Africa. Those who enlisted would serve as orderlies to their officers. I explained the options to Tomasi, urging him to return to Kenya rather than enlist, for there would now be insufficient time to give him other than basic training. Tomasi, though, saw in the order the greatest opportunity of his life: to be an askari of the KAR. We argued, we discussed. Tomasi was adamant: he would enlist to stay with me. I knew when I was beaten. Of the battalion's forty-five personal servants, just four enlisted. Tomasi became No. N/40605 Private Thomas Liech, 36 (Tanganyika Territory) Battalion, The King's African Rifles. His Army paybook, his AB64, stated it in black and white. Triumphantly he wrote home to his mother and father, and to the girl named Serafina.

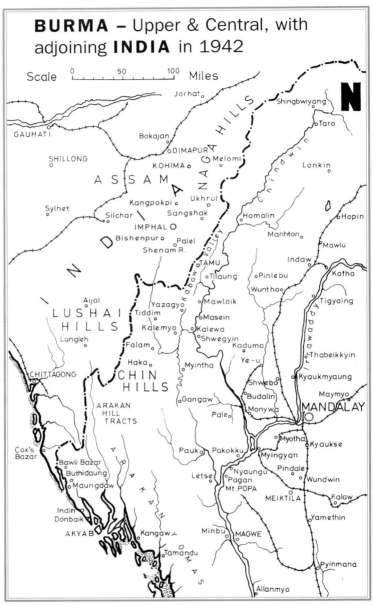

BURMA – Upper & Central, with adjoining INDIA in 1942

Scale 0 ___ 50 ___ 100 Miles

Jorhat

Shingbwiyang

Taro

GAUHATI

Bokajan

DIMAPUR

SHILLONG

KOHIMA

Melomi

Lonkin

NAGA HILLS

ASSAM

Chindwin

Sylhet

Kangpokpi

Ukhrul

Silchar

Sangshak

Homalin

Hopin

IMPHAL

Manhton

Bishenpur

Palel

Mawlu

Shenam R.

Indaw

TAMU

Tilaung

Pinlebu

Katha

Wunthoo

Kabaw Valley

INDIA

Aijal

Yazagyo

Mawlaik

Tigyaing

LUSHAI

Tiddim

Masein

HILLS

Kalemyo

Kalewa

Lungleh

Shwegyin

Falam

Kaduma

Irrawaddy

Ye-u

Thabeikkyin

CHITTAGONG

Haka

Myintha

Kyaukmyaung

CHIN

Shwebo

HILLS

Budalin

Maymyo

Gangaw

Monywa

MANDALAY

ARAKAN

HILL

Pale

TRACTS

Cox's

Myotha

Kyaukse

Bazar

Pauk

Pakokku

Myingyan

Bawli Bazar

Nyaungu

Pindale

Buthidaung

Letse

Pagan

Wundwin

Maungdaw

Mt.POPA

MEIKTILA

Kalaw

ARAKAN

Indin

Yamethin

Donbaik

AKYAB

Kangaw

Minbu

MAGWE

YOMAS

Tamandu

Pyinmana

Allanmyo

Map of Burma by Norman Havers, first published in *Tales from the Burma Campaign 1942– 1945*, (1998). Reproduced with kind permission of the Burma Campaign Fellowship Group.

The Valley

THE SOUTH-WEST MONSOON was at its height when the huge, multi-deck sternwheel paddle-steamer carrying the battalion thrashed up the wide Brahmaputra River to Gauhati in Assam. Two weeks later we were on the road to Mandalay, spearheading 14 Army's advance south down the Kabaw Valley. Infested with malaria and scrub typhus, the Kabaw is a depression of dense teak forest drenched with unceasing downpours of torrential rain. The valley floor is from 10 to 20 miles wide and flanked by high mountain ranges. To the east, over the mountains, lies the mighty Chindwin River, running parallel to the valley from north to south. From the mountains on either side several rivers and a multitude of chaungs run across the track, which they intersect every few hundred yards; all are full and fast-flowing and many of them in spate during the long, monsoon months.

The Japanese Army was now in full retreat, General Mutaguchi's grand strategic plan for the invasion of India destroyed at the battles of Imphal and Kohima. The great offensive had been launched in March, only weeks before the onset of the monsoon, in anticipation of a swift victory to be consolidated when, the Japanese High Command believed – wrongly, as they were to find to their cost – the rains must bring large-scale war-waging to a virtual standstill. A second optimistic assumption of crucial importance was that their victorious army would live off the conquered fertile land and from captured food dumps. First halted, then soundly defeated and prevented from seizing India's crops and foodstores, the previously unthinkable retreat became inevitable. Because retreat was unthinkable, there was no contingency plan to meet it. Air supply to their hard-pressed troops on the ground was not possible: the Japanese Air Force was built on fighter aircraft, not bombers and not at all on cargo-carriers with parachute- and free-drop capability. In any case, the Royal Air Force and the Indian Air Force now had mastery of the skies over Burma.

With their supply vehicles mired hopelessly to the axles in the Kabaw's deep mud and their meat-on-the-hoof cattle herds long since eaten or lost, Japanese quartermasters employed reserve troops as a human supply-chain. Moving only under cover of darkness, to escape attention from strafing and bombing fighter aircraft, long columns of men made their way nightly to the front line carrying balls of cooked rice wrapped in leaves to sustain their comrades in their desperate fighting. The rice bowl of India now an unattainable goal and the spectre of starvation staring them in the face, units began to falter in their resolve. Others, though, retained their cohesion and were brought together in order to delay the British advance and give Burma Area Army Command vital time to regroup.

Thousands of Japanese were killed before the order was given on 31 May to fall back to the Chindwin River. With this the long retreat began. The surviving sick and wounded were told to make their way as best they could, many dying by the roadside when their last reserves of strength failed as they struggled up the succession of steep hills on the long trek. Hundreds more died in the burnt wreckage of buildings blasted by air attack. At Tamu, at the head of the Kabaw Valley, the pagoda was filled with Japanese who had crawled there to die at the foot of the four tall, golden statues of Buddha, surrounded by abandoned steel helmets, field service packs, rifles, hand grenades, and other paraphernalia of war.

To the retreating Japanese forces June, July, and August were an endless nightmare of agony and despair as we pursued them in their struggle towards the Chindwin. The Kabaw, no picnic-spot at the best of times, becomes a green, waterlogged hell from May to October. Starving, because there was no longer even the pretence of a supply-chain, human or otherwise; suffering from beri-beri, dysentery, scrub typhus, and malaria; and with thousands of untreated wounded, ever-

greater numbers of men lay down to die. Uniformed bodies
and skeletons sprawled on the soaking ground, many with
limbs bandaged or in plaster-casts. Some soldiers had thrown
down pairs of groundsheets just a yard or two from the muddy
track to fulfil a death pact made with a comrade: one would
shoot the other before turning the gun on himself. Others blew
themselves up with a hand-grenade clasped to the chest.
Glossy black scalps lay inside khaki field service caps, separated from the skull by decomposition. Clusters of writhing maggots feasted on the wounds of the dying and in the eye-sockets
and mouths of the dead. Sated flies lay like a black cloth on the
bodies that had fed them; swarms of hungry flies hummed
ceaselessly overhead as they waited for their place at the table.

In groups of ramshackle grass huts, on makeshift beds, and
on the floor, the wounded, the sick, and the starving had taken
shelter, begging for rescue by passing comrades or pleading to
be killed. But their comrades were too weak, too desperate for
their own survival, beyond all caring, and staggered on wildly
down the track. Strewn over gaseous, bloated bodies family
photographs, postcards of cherry-blossom and snowcapped
Mount Fujiyama and delicate drawings of flowers had fallen
from dying hands as life ebbed away in the roar of the unceasing rains. The stench of putrefaction and gangrene hung over
the jungle in a sickly cloud. Down narrow, winding tracks
threading their uncertain way through the deep, green jungle
barely-human remnants of Japanese fighting units reeled without hope, seeing one after another of their comrades fall and
die. It had taken them weeks to get this far and few would survive to see the waters of the Chindwin.

Retreat can bring instant death in rearguard skirmish and
slower death from mortal wounds. Its companions are starvation and disease and the final collapse of the human spirit. In
retreat death comes to the soldier who falls beside the narrow
track and is too weak to rise yet again to his feet; and it waits
for him as he shelters in the cab of an abandoned truck, pray-
ing for the help that never comes. Death creeps upon the starving, shaking, rain-sodden creature which has tried and failed

to survive for weeks on grass and roots. It comes from drowning in the raging waters of swollen chaungs which bar the seemingly endless path to safety, and lies in wait for those too weak to attempt another crossing. In the huge loneliness of the jungle violent death comes at the hands of half-naked, demented soldiers turned into hunting packs killing the weak and robbing the dead for a last handful of mouldy rice.

In terms of the scale of human suffering the Imperial Japanese Army's retreat from Imphal and Kohima must rank alongside such epics as Napoleon's retreat from Moscow and that of the beaten German armies from Stalingrad in the Second World War. In all three of these catastrophic defeats lines of communication had been stretched until they broke; food supplies failed; and appalling weather conditions added a third, fatal dimension. The generals – French, German, Japanese – had brushed aside such possibilities as pessimistic in their euphoric expectation of quick victory which would solve problems of feeding and sustaining their armies. By the end of the war in Burma 180,000 Japanese soldiers would have lost their lives in almost four years of campaigning.

Fresh in the field the KAR's advance was along a track which, unmetalled and narrow, was designated on the map as a car road with a cautionary note: 'impassable to vehicles during the monsoon months.' Improbably, this was the main road from Dimapur in Assam to Mandalay. From Tamu it ran south for 70 miles to Kalemyo, and beyond to Kalewa on the Chindwin River, crowded by primary and secondary jungle whose occasional open areas allowed rice paddy-field cultivation by peasants living in the villages which lay on either side of it. Throughout the monsoon the jungle-clad mountain ranges towering over the valley floor were shrouded in black, rain-laden clouds, a deadly hazard lying in wait for the Army's low-flying fighter support and supply-dropping aircraft. The rains had turned the track into a river of mud so deep that wheeled vehicles had to be manhandled yard by yard by infantry askaris. As conditions worsened the entire battalion spent a month as roadbuilders, felling countless thousands of young

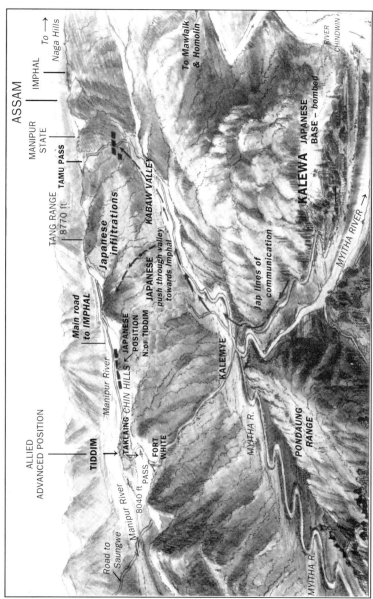

Panoramic drawing of operations in north Burma showing attempted
Japanese invasion of north-east India, March 1944; published in *Sphere*
on 8 April 1944. © Illustrated London News Picture Library

trees and laying the slender trunks lengthwise to form a 'corduroy road' to restore the supply-line and allow the gunners to bring up their 25-pounders and 3.7 in. howitzers. When the track became completely impassable to vehicles the Royal Air Force and United States Air Force began to fly in supplies. Every few days Dropping Zones were selected and prepared for parachute and free-drop, markers for the pilots laid out and troops organised in collection work-parties to dash out the minute the last Dakota and 'Commando' aircraft had roared away to India to load up for another sortie. This was half-ration time.

Reports of Japanese movements on the valley floor and in the hills coming in from Force 136's hidden watching-posts called for continuous patrolling to discover enemy strength and intentions. Parties of Japanese stragglers were hunted down and killed as they resisted to the end or slipped away into the jungle, bravely persisting in their struggle to reach the distant Chindwin. A KAR patrol sent to Dathwekyauk Atet, a remote village high in the hills to the east, came under machine-gun and rifle fire from a determined enemy and a platoon commander was mortally wounded in the fierce little battle that followed. It was plainly dangerous and self-deluding to believe that the retreating Japanese could offer little resistance to a well-fed, well-armed advancing enemy. Those still with the physical strength to do so fought all the harder to avoid the ultimate disgrace of capture, for a Japanese soldier taken prisoner 'ceased to exist' and could never return to his homeland and his family. His duty and his reward were to die for the Emperor. Tenno Heika Banzai! May the Emperor live ten thousand years!

★ ★ ★

Japanese Private Manabu Wada was one of those thousands struggling along 'Human Remains Road' towards the Chindwin. Back in mid-March, in the dry season, his 138 Infantry Regiment had waded across the shallow Chindwin at Tamanthe to spearhead the Retsu 'Irresistible Force' Legion's advance on Kohima. With no thought of defeat, only of victory, they marched out with twenty days' rations and a herd of cattle as their meat-on-the-hoof towards their destiny beyond the jungle-covered mountain range. They found the conditions hard. At 9,000 feet the mountains were shrouded in freezing cloud, the rocks and trees covered in moss and lichen. Matches struck at this altitude immediately went out through lack of oxygen so that there was no possibility of lighting fires to boil rice or cook meat. To make matters worse, the pack mules fell down cliffsides so steep that the troops could not descend to retrieve the lost supplies; and many of the cattle fell to join the mules. The bodies of British and Indian soldiers who had died of wounds or disease as they retreated in the face of the Japanese advance lay along the track, corpses blown up with gas gangrene as they decomposed.

Among themselves the Japanese soldiers complained bitterly of the incompetence of the generals who had sent them over the mountains without proper climbing gear, clothing, or equipment and hampered by cattle unable to negotiate the steep, rocky paths which even the troops found difficult enough. At last, though, the regiment reached the summit and could see Tibet and the Himalayas to the west, across a boundless ocean of clouds. Buoyed up, they pressed forward towards Kohima. Following prolonged, bitter fighting the regiment captured Kohima Ridge late in April but by now their rations were completely exhausted. The British had burned their food and supply depots so that 'not even a grain of rice was left for us'. All that Private Wada and his mates could find were three tins of corned beef left behind in abandoned enemy trenches. How, they asked their officers, could they be expected to fight on without food? Their division had been promised ten tonnes a day after the 'Imphal Project' began but now, as April entered its third week, still nothing had come. Three tins of corned beef and a few biscuits could not sustain them.

The British artillery's heavy and medium shells in their thousands rained down on them, great barrages which were a prelude to one infantry attack after another. For their part, the Japanese gunners were limited to just a few shells each day in

British psychological warfare 'encouragement to surrender' leaflet dropped by the Royal Air Force over Japanese positions at Yazagyo, Kabaw Valley, July 1944. The leaflet was recovered after a small action by Lieutenant G. A. 'Sam' Shepperson, 13 (Nyasaland) Battalion, King's African Rifles. A translation is given on the facing page.

Fifty thousand corpses – your comrades – are now being stripped clean on the rolling hills of Burma, where all that can be heard is the sound of the wind blowing over the dreams of your commanders.

The jungle grasses may shelter the bones of your comrades from the wind, but the inefficiency of your commanders is inexhaustible.

THE BURMA DREAMS ARE OVER

Defeat in Battle, retreat, starvation, death – this is what lies ahead of you.

JAPANESE SOLDIERS!

Once again, with your inferior weapons, you have been ordered to stand and face the Allied armies who are armed with first-rate modern weapons. How can you save the lives you value when you are face to face with a mountain of weapons, flame-throwers, heavy tanks and aircraft? You are about to repeat the same story as when you retreated across the Chindwin River. With what eyes will you gaze upon your commanders who have destroyed you and brought death to so many thousands of true and brave Japanese soldiers, when you lie in heaps of dead just like your comrades who went to their deaths continually tormented by maggots and white ants, and who were left behind in the jungle?

Your commanders are devising operational plans in the belief they can halt us; but just as they were powerless to stop us at Imphal, at Kohima, at Ukhrul, at Tamu, at Myitkina, they have now no means of any kind; they realise full well they have no impetus left to stop our offensive.

JAPANESE SOLDIERS!
THE DREAM IS OVER

On the reverse side of the leaflet, with an illustration showing skulls and helmets lying in a jungle scene, is Sasho's famous poem, the same quoted in the book *Sittang* as epigraph:

Natsu-gusa ya   Summer grasses . . .
tauwamono-domo no   all that is left of
yuma no ato   the dreams of warriors

the continuing failure of supplies to come up from the rear. It was only at around three o'clock in the afternoons, when the British took a tea-break, that there was any respite from the bursting shells. The Japanese soldiers watched helplessly as their enemy brewed and drank their tea out of rifle range. On 18 April Wada's commmanding officer had blown himself up by lying on a hand grenade, no longer able to bear the strain. Sadly and with a growing sense of despair his men cut off his hands and burned them so that the bones might be preserved for consecration at the Yasukuni Shrine in Tokyo. Morale was sinking fast in the terror of the storms of shrapnel which burst above them with tremendous force and jagged shards of steel which ripped off heads and legs and arms and ploughed through torsos. Without food, without rifle and machine-gun ammunition, and lacking artillery and air support, the Retsu Legion fought desperately as the monsoon rains began their months' long deluge.

Even if there had been rice to eat no fires could be lit and kept going in the rain. Just once in a while, in a brief respite, a fire stayed alight and the soldiers managed to boil vegetable matter rooted from the ground as the only means of staving off their terrible hunger. When the shelling became too intense they entered their octopus traps – holes dug in the ground to a man's height – but the rain flooded in so that almost at once they were standing chest-high in water and had to climb out and take their chance against the shelling. When at last the order was given to retreat to the Chindwin the remnants of 138 Regiment straggled away from the battlefield. Of 3,800 men who had started out on 15 March just a few hundred now survived. Without shelter from the never-ending rains, with boots that had long since rotted so that now they were bound with grass, the starving, broken soldiers began their trudge along the deep mud paths, carrying rifles without ammunition and leaning on sticks to support their weak bodies. Stretcher-bearers slipped and slid and fell as they carried the sick and wounded over the seemingly endless mountains. When a man cried out again in agony stretcher-bearers at the end of their tether would shout, 'If you complain any more, we'll make it easy for you' – and throw both stretcher and soldier down the cliffside.

Once Wada and three companions found a tent in the jungle and entered it to shelter from the icy rain which pierced them to the marrow. Inside the tent were the bodies of some nurses. Why, they asked themselves, had the nurses not been taken to a place of safety? How could they have been left to die in this wilderness? In another tent nearby lay the bodies of ten soldiers who had killed themselves or, by pact, one another until the last man took his own life. Manabu Wada swore to himself that, somehow, he would survive. And in an epic of human suffering and endurance he did survive. With three comrades he reached the Chindwin and built a raft of bamboo that drifted them a hundred miles downriver to safety at Kalewa.

★ ★ ★

Accidents don't just happen, more often than not their origins lie in a human act of omission or commission. In the case of the accident that befell Lieutenant McKean, the starting-point of a sequence of ever-worsening events was a hasty, ill-considered order by our highly volatile commanding officer, who sent him out late one afternoon on an impossible mission. The battalion had received orders to lead the 'push' down the valley and an advance party moved along the main track to select a suitable new location. There was a need to warn the Patiala Regiment, dug-in at a river junction 8 miles away on the flank, of our arrival, and McKean, the Battalion Intelligence Officer, was ordered to go by Jeep with a corporal and three askaris. The patrol made slow going along the narrow, muddy track pitted with potholes and scored by deep ruts which wound its way though the jungle. The monsoon rains had turned the valley floor into a sheet of water deep enough to cover the track completely in places and this slowed progress still further. It soon became obvious that travel by shanks's pony would get the patrol to the Patialas sooner than any Jeep but 'orders is orders' and they struggled on as best they could. At about halfway the Jeep sank yet again axle-deep in the mud and this time no amount of manhandling could extricate it. With another 4 miles still to go McKean decided that he and an Intelligence Section askari would go on by foot, leaving the other three to guard the Jeep. He reasoned that two men would make faster and quieter progress than five but even so they would be lucky if they managed 2 miles an hour in the dark; in any case he was unwilling to abandon the Jeep until a party could recover it the next day.

Soon it was night, dark but not pitch-black, and the two men advanced slowly and as silently as they could among the tall trees and thick undergrowth. All was quiet except for the usual nocturnal jungle noises and then, at last, came the sound of flowing waters suggesting that the Patialas' riverbank positions were now nearby. Having carried out his orders thus far McKean pondered how he might safely attract attention as friend, not foe, for there was a real danger that they could be mistaken for a night-raiding Japanese jitter-party probing the defences. In training we had been taught that one way of doing so was to put our bush hat on a stick and lift it high from behind solid cover but in the dark this was scarcely an option. What best to do? A sudden burst of machine-gun fire from close range split the silence and McKean fell, shot in the leg. From his askari there was no sound: he could be dead or at best unconscious. No further firing occurred but the Patialas – he had to assume it was the Patialas and not Japanese – must be peering into the jungle from their slit-trenches and would take no chances if they heard the slightest noise. Besides, they would know, as we did, that the Japanese often called out tauntingly in English or pretended they were wounded British soldiers begging for rescue.

For about half-an-hour McKean waited and watched and listened in vain before deciding he must try to rejoin the rest of the patrol. Somehow or another – miraculously without attracting renewed attention – he got to his feet and made his way painfully back the way he had come, only to find the Jeep had been abandoned. The corporal and the two askaris must have decided to return to the advance party rather than stay out all night. There was nothing for it but to struggle on for another 4 miles in the hope of reaching our positions without encountering any Japanese lurking on the track. As dawn broke his luck turned and he came across a KAR post, from which he was quickly evacuated to a casualty clearing station. He was found to have a .303 in. Bren gun bullet lodged – extraordinarily – between the bones of his right lower leg, one of the bones being fractured. Presumably his boot had taken some of the bullet's force. Later that day the Patialas returned the askari, whom they had found at dawn outside their perimeter. He had been shot in the thigh and, like McKean, was thoroughly aggrieved at being wounded by 'friendly fire'.

The colonel's order was little short of madness. To send out at that late hour a small, lightly-armed patrol with a Jeep to cover 8 miles in the short time before darkness fell, along an unknown, waterlogged track, with the danger of encountering enemy troops, was bad enough. Moreover, the racket made by the Jeep's engine would alert any Japanese in the vicinity to 'easy pickings', thus compounding the potential for disaster. What made matters even worse was that no radio contact with the Patialas had been attempted in order to warn them of the patrol's approach and agree a password and meeting-point. A strong fighting patrol should have undertaken the task, leaving at first light so as to be able to return in daylight – but lieutenants know that theirs is not to reason why. One man's misfortune, though, is another man's good luck: I was at once appointed to replace McKean as Intelligence Officer.

Initially I had mixed feelings about my new job. Shortly before we were due to leave for Burma I had been on a 3-in. mortar course at Saugor, in India's United Provinces, where I learned all about these powerful and effective close-support weapons. As boys in our early teens I and Robin and Tom Atkinson, the Long Buckby village doctor's two younger sons, spent happy hours playing with gunpowder extracted from firework 'bangers' or purchased, 'Eight ounces of gunpowder, please, Mr Browning', from the ironmonger and tamped into the barrels of our toy field guns which then fired deadly projectiles to decimate the ranks of our opposing lead soldier armies. The pall of acrid smoke from these artillery barrages hung over the battlefield in satisfyingly realistic, nostril-delighting fashion. With these impressive pre-war explosives qualifications, I was delighted to be appointed second-in-command of the Mortar Platoon on my return from Saugor. I could now play with big boys' toys to my heart's content, albeit against an enemy who, regrettably, could fire back at me.

Real-life war, Robin, Tom, and I were finding, was very different from those childhood games played in the cavernous lofts of the old Northamptonshire-sandstone outbuildings bordering Holly House's drive. Robin, who had joined the Royal Air Force in 1937 on a short-service commission, went down in his Spitfire when another aircraft in the low-level formation came from below and the two collided. There was no time to bale out. With appalling burns and disfiguring injuries he spent two years at East Grinstead as one of Sir Archibald MacIndoe's 'guinea-pigs' before being passed fit again for operational flying, a hero by the most exacting standards. After many successful sorties Tom's Typhoon failed to return from ground-attacking over Northern France, his wingman reporting that both fighters flew into cloud at altitude and Tom's was never seen again. (Typhoons' oxygen system was notoriously unreliable, with often-fatal consequences for the pilot.) Their brother, Jack, was wounded when his Northamptonshire Yeomanry tank was knocked out in a battle in north-west Europe.

Training, that continuous requirement and process which enables posts made vacant through death, wounds, sickness and promotion more readily to be filled by well-rounded officers and men, had occupied all our time. In common with others I had been on a wide variety of courses and was considered fully-trained for most tasks that lay ahead of the battalion. My unexpected and sudden translation as the unfortunate McKean's replacement proved entirely painless for, somewhat to my surprise, I found that this new post fitted my temperament and leanings so perfectly it might have been tailormade for me. I also had the satisfaction of knowing that the Intelligence Section was a well-trained unit. At the same time, though, I was disappointed that I would not be going into action with the mortars unless – or until – the platoon commander became a casualty, when I could expect my captaincy out of it.

With the Intelligence Section leading the way I accompanied 'C' Company on a strong fighting patrol led by its commander, Ted Onslow. Ted had fought with distinction in Abyssinia, winning the Military Cross, and was a man of powerful personality, a born, no-nonsense leader who knew with absolute certainty that his askaris would follow him into the cannon's mouth. Where many other Kenya farmers had returned to their farms after the Abyssinian Campaign, to increase food production, Ted and a very few others stayed with the battalion.

At Mile 10 from Tamu we cautiously entered a village close to the track and searched the houses for any Japanese who might be hiding in them. At the far end of the village a small shrine beneath a rusted corrugated-iron roof housed a statue of Buddha gazing out across the paddy-fields. Lying at the foot of the Buddha was a naked Japanese soldier, a barely-living skeleton, with an empty water bottle at his side. Glaring wildly at us he croaked some words before his head fell back on to the mud floor. Buddha is compassionate. Why then had not the villagers nursed the straggler, fed him, given him water? Every man, woman, and child would have watched him as he baked and starved and thirsted under the corrugated-iron, too weak even to fill his water bottle from the rain cascading down the sides of the shrine. He may well have been dying as much from dehydration as from disease, for in this condition water passes straight through the body, whose cells are no longer able to absorb it. Perilously far gone though he was, we hoped that he might survive and sent him back with medical orderlies guarded by an askari escort. A few days later a signal from headquarters told us that he had died. The sense of sadness and almost personal loss that I felt at the news was to stay with me, for I was discovering that it is one thing to kill in the heat of battle and another to see a man dying from wounds, disease, and starvation who might have been saved, perhaps by one's own actions.

The dying man's ravings in delirium had been written down by a Japanese-speaking intelligence officer and a copy was later sent to us, for it was only very rarely that an officer fell into British hands. In his book, *Monsoon Victory*, Gerald Hanley records those last words: 'Lieutenant Hazaki! Lieutenant Hazaki, where are you, you bastard? Shoot me with your pistol! Come and shoot me! You useless fool! For the sake of the Emperor we came to these filthy hills to be disgraced. Dragged on my behind by blackamoors! We came from Indo-China to be disgraced and clowned by blackamoors. Lieutenant Hazaki, you bastard, bring a machine-gun and mow them down! Our useless bloody soldiers. Hazaki, turn the machine-gun on these useless Japanese soldiers! Ah, the disgrace. A Japanese officer dragged in the mud. Hey, are you there, Hazaki? Shoot me! Shoot me! God save the Emperor! Tenno Haika Banzai! Koroshito Kure! Shoot me!'

A day or two later a report came in that a lone Japanese had been seen to the south of our area and I took the 'I' Section to find him. We moved off in close order down the track, two scouts out in front with their eyes skinned for any sign of our quarry. It was not long before I saw the leading scout 'freeze', and the second scout dart into the tall, trackside grass to make his way back to report that a Japanese in uniform and a Burman were approaching. Quickly laying an ambush, I was confident that we as good as had the pair in our grasp. I intended to try to capture them alive for interrogation by Divisional Intelligence and planned that we would simply rush out from concealment and seize them both. Disaster! In his excitement an askari accidentally fired his rifle. Leading a headlong charge I raced up the track as the two men vanished into the undergrowth but although we fanned out and searched the area on both sides of the track we had been given the slip. The jungle can be a friendly place – but this time it was friendly to the wrong people. As for the hapless askari, I decided that all I could do do was to give him a fierce dressing-down and hope that he and the rest of the Intelligence Section had learnt a sharp lesson from the fiasco. The sequel came the next day.

Once again the Japanese soldier had been sighted, this time close to 'B' Company's perimeter, and Lieutenant Goode went off with his platoon to find and bring him in or kill him. Bootprints in the mud made tracking easy and it was not long before the platoon encircled a small area in which he was hiding. As the askaris closed in on him he leapt to his feet and fired a single shot that brought Goode down before dying in a storm of shooting. Examination showed that he was a captain. In his pocket I found a sketch-map of the long route that he had followed during the previous three weeks from which it was clear that he was on an important reconnaissance mission. There was no doubt that he was the man who had escaped my ambush attempt. I cursed the askari who had denied me my prize and indirectly caused us another officer-casualty.

A white man amongst black soldiers was always the prime target of Japanese fire: killing the leader makes sound military sense. All Europeans now coated their faces and hands with black cream and removed rank badges before leaving the perimeter on patrols which went out every day to seek the enemy, protect our flanks, and clear small pockets of resistance wherever they were found. A black-painted face was not enough, though, to save Company Sergeant-Major O'Hara, ambushed on a fighting patrol. He and his askaris fought back bravely, killing eight Japanese, but tragedy followed immediately: one of the Japanese feigned death and while O'Hara was turning him over the 'dead' man – an officer – killed him with a single pistol shot before leaping to his feet and dashing into the jungle. After that bitter lesson in warfare no chances were taken.

Reports came in that as many as fifty Japanese and Indian National Army soldiers were occupying Witok, a large village 3 miles to the east. This would be our first encounter with the

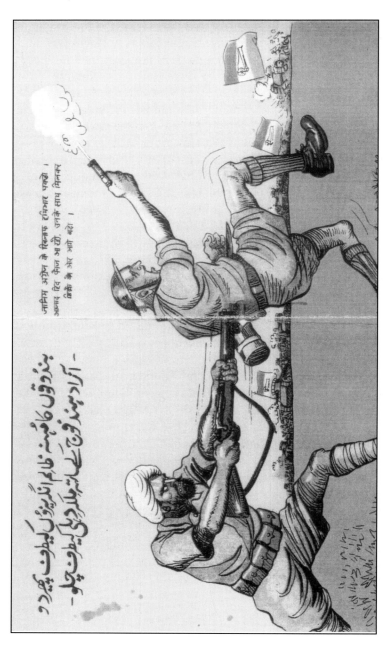

'Traitor Army' formed by Subhas Chandra Bose, leader of the Indian National Congress party, of Indian Army soldiers taken prisoner throughout the Far East and encouraged or persuaded to fight on the side of the Japanese to liberate India from British imperialism. Already we had abundant evidence of the INA presence nearby: nominal rolls of men serving in the Azad Brigade and the Gandhi Brigade had been found in several villages and sent back to intelligence officers concerned to assess the strength of the INA and identify Indian Army defectors. The INA was said to comprise 10,000 former Indian Army soldiers and 20,000 civilian volunteers, a force which represented a considerable threat after the Japanese had invaded and occupied Burma.

The Japanese Government had had the foresight to realise the importance of having a military alliance with an independent India, Subhas Chandra Bose's ultimate objective, and encouraged the formation of the INA following the British surrender of Singapore on 15 February 1942. It was not until mid-1943, however, that the full potential of the INA dawned on the Japanese. Invited to Tokyo, Chandra Bose proclaimed the 'Free India Provisional Government' and made a declaration of war against Britain. The next day, in Singapore, he took the salute at an INA march-past. It so happened that the Japanese Prime Minister, General Tojo, was also in Singapore. Standing on the dais with Bose he recognised at once the immense value of a greatly expanded INA in an invasion and occupation of Assam. To the immense satisfaction of Chandra Bose the Prime Minister declared that 1 INA Division was to be prepared for action in Burma. At this early stage in the game there was wild enthusiasm amongst the INA troops, many

Facing page Indian National Army propaganda leaflet dropped by the Japanese Air Force over Allied positions on the Tiddim Road. Found in the jungle by Captain Tom Bruin, 7th/10th Baluch Regiment, Indian Army.

Translation 'Take up arms against the accursed English! The Free Indian Army is coming – join up with them and go forward against their [*sic*] English positions!'

seeing themselves as heroes in the struggle for their country's liberation from British rule. Their rallying cry, 'Jai Hind! Chalo Delhi!' 'India for ever! On to Delhi!' was to ring hollow as one defeat after another sent morale plunging, and the retreat from Kohima and Imphal put an end to the INA as an organised fighting force. From then on its stragglers would join in the agonising struggle to reach the Chindwin.

A two-company dawn attack on Witok was ordered, to be led by the battalion's second-in-command, Major Marsh of the Suffolks. Leaving our defensive perimeter at two o'clock in the morning we made our way in closed-up single file along muddy, rain-soaked tracks, slipping, stumbling, silently cursing as the column splashed through streams and forded thigh-deep, fast-flowing chaungs. In the pitch dark it was impossible to see anything but the bulk of the man in front as we tripped and fell again and again over projecting tree roots and on slimy rocks. Brought down headlong by an object lying in a chaung Major Astell found it was a Samurai sword, its blade intricately engraved by a master-craftsman of centuries past. It was not difficult to imagine the feelings of the Japanese officer who threw away his cherished heirloom as a burden he no longer had the strength to carry.

By five o'clock we were in position outside the village, undetected. Either the enemy had not posted sentries or we had in some miraculous way avoided them, and as dawn lightened the sky we closed on the stilt-houses and enfiladed the pathways running between them. The signal for the attack – a green Verey light fired into the sky followed by prolonged bursts of automatic fire aimed away from houses to avoid civilian casualties – sent two platoons charging into the village. From out of a dozen houses tumbled INA soldiers in all states of undress, hands above their heads in surrender. Some of the Japanese were shot down as they tried to escape into the jungle, others were killed in pathways between the houses. None survived the attack.

Not all the thirty captured INA soldiers – 'Japanese Indian Forces', as the INA was also known – were Indians. The majority was Sikh but there were several Koreans who must have volunteered for the INA or been impressed. One prisoner, surprisingly, was a Gurkha; for him the disgrace he had brought upon himself and his family meant that there could be no return to his home village. All seemed to have lost the will to fight, even though they looked well fed in comparison with the Japanese, but it was as well to remember that appearances can be deceptive, especially in circumstances such as a surprise dawn attack. There was no doubting that if the boot had been on the other foot, so to speak, the INA would have taken no prisoners for fear of being identified after the war and shot as traitors.

Sergeant Makinde Mosi of the 'I' Section called me to see a Japanese soldier standing upright but stone-dead against a shoulder-height woven fence, his legs in a running stride. He had died instantly, in full flight, wearing only his trousers. Laying him on the ground I searched his pockets for a paybook and identification papers but there was nothing. On his wrist, though, he was wearing an Ingersoll watch with the initials 'JB' scratched deeply on the back. Who was 'JB'? A British soldier killed at Kohima or Imphal, perhaps? As I put the watch in a haversack, to be sent to rear headquarters with other captured items and papers, I felt we had evened the score for 'JB'. The following night we went off to launch a dawn attack on Sunle, another large village where more Japanese and INA were reported by Burmese to be sheltering. This time we wounded and captured a Japanese artillery captain and took thirteen JIFs prisoner, again with no casualties on our part. These proved to be the last remnants of the Indian National Army we would encounter: from now on all our fighting would be against the Japanese, who were reported to be preparing 'defence-and-delay' operations in the valley. Of the 10,000 INA soldiers who had paraded before Subhas Chandra Bose and General Tojo in Singapore, 750 were killed and 5,000 deserted. The rest died of disease or were captured. Their military record was to be one of outstanding failure.

My solitary afternoon walks in Somaliland and elsewhere

should have given me enough alarming experiences to deter me from ever again going off on my own, let alone doing so in the Burma jungle in campaign conditions, but old habits die hard and as Intelligence Officer I convinced myself that it was my duty to check out Maw, a nearby riparian village. The thought that I might run into Japanese or Indian National Army troops barely entered my head as I set off to follow a track running eastwards to the village which lay on a broad, sweeping bend of the Yu River 2 miles away. I was well-armed: Sten gun with five magazines, revolver, and four hand grenades. I could take care of myself.

The rain had stopped and I enjoyed walking through the light, secondary jungle, stopping every so often to take stock before venturing further, but all was quiet, even serene – the sort of tranquillity I sometimes craved. Soon I came across a heavily-trampled pool area where elephants washed; the foliage up to fifteen feet or so high was smothered in mud from their squirting and larking about. The sight of this gave me enormous pleasure so that for a moment or two I could imagine myself a peacetime traveller in remote Burma, a plant collector, perhaps, or manager of a teak forest operation on a tour of inspection. Still further on the wreck of a Japanese Type 97 two-man tankette lay beside the track, minus its 37 mm gun. It was impossible to guess how long it had been there but its presence alerted my senses and reminded me of my vulnerability. As soon as the first houses came into view, I lay up in the jungle and watched for any movement for a good fifteen minutes before approaching a little closer, ready to dart into hiding at the slightest sign of trouble.

It began to dawn on me that other perils besides Japanese and Indian National Army troops might be lurking along the track. We had learned that early in 1941 the Burma nationalist, Aung San, had made a clandestine visit to Tokyo, returning with an offer to support an uprising against the British and train a hand-picked group of young men in Japan to form the officer nucleus of a liberation army. Since their return from Japan these dedicated followers had become known as 'The

Thirty Comrades' committed to rid their country of the kalahe, 'the foreigners from the West'. With Aung San as leader, the Burma Independence Army was launched later that year and began its preparations to fight alongside the Japanese ally with the ultimate promised goal of independence. The opportunity soon came: during our retreat to India in 1942 the BIA hunted down and killed British and Indian soldiers, Ba Maw, a leader with Aung San, trumpeting, 'The boys were jubilant at the thought of having drawn white blood so cheaply!' Detachments of the Burma National Army, as it was now known, sheltering in villages on our flanks would regard a solitary British soldier as fair game. In spite of my misgivings and against all common sense I continued my jungle promenade, determined to check Maw and see the Yu.

As I walked between the first houses-on-stilts I caught a breathtaking view from the high, sloping riverbank to the far side, across the wide, fast-running brown waters. At first I thought the village must be empty; it was too neat and tidy to be deserted. As I watched, an old woman wandered out from beneath one of the houses and stared at me before turning towards the river and shouting a warning to invisible villagers on the far bank. I decided it was time to leave. If any straggler Japanese or JIFs were sheltering in the village they would be after me like a shot and if by some really bad luck a cohesive enemy unit was in occupation I could find myself in a tricky situation. The villagers themselves might capture a lone soldier and hand him over to the Japanese. I beat a hasty and, as it turned out, uneventful retreat, once again resolving that I would give up my lone ventures.

A day or two later I learned that I was not the only one who went off alone into the jungle. Disguised as a Burman, whether convincingly or not who can say, a major from divisional headquarters left our perimeter on a lone intelligence mission. His orders were to visit villages which lay south along the track in no man's land and gather information about the enemy's strength and condition. He was never seen again. Did he die a lonely death similar to that of the Japanese captain who had shot Lieutenant Goode? I had to admit to myself that there was an important difference between the major's mission and mine: he was bravely doing his duty and I was merely indulging a foolhardy habit I seemed unable to shake off.

Patrol to Panma Taung

THE MONSOON had just about rained itself dry and the warm, early October morning made one glad to be alive. Of course, there were those who claimed that there were many places they would rather be in at that moment than Burma but I wasn't going to let them spoil my enjoyment of the day ahead. Nor did I in the least mind when the suggestion, more an order, was put to me over breakfast that I might care to lead a reconnaissance patrol to find out whether a major hill feature some 5 miles away was home to the Japanese or offered vacant possession. I joked that a there-and-back 'constitutional' of 10 miles along the floor of the Kabaw Valley should be a comfortable distance. A longer walk might prove tiring, I pointed out.

The Kabaw had earned its other name of Death Valley. During the British Army's epic 1942 retreat northwards up the Kabaw, pursued by the Japanese invaders sweeping towards the Indian border, thousands of Burmese and Indian refugees and many troops died from its endemic diseases and from dysentery, starvation, and physical and mental exhaustion. The continuing presence two years later of the Imperial Japanese Army's soldiers of almost fanatical bravery and an awesome readiness to die for their Emperor added another dimension to the valley's reputation. For all that, I had found the Kabaw an interesting place in which to spend a little time .

I was selective in my choice of askaris to accompany me. I had been almost three years, on and off, with the battalion and knew the men with whom I would be most confident: Sergeant Makinde Mosi and Privates Wambunyu, Lugembe, Mohammed, Rajabu, and Juma. We made scrupulously careful preparation for our patrol. Everything we needed was cleaned and inspected: Sten gun with five magazines and Smith &

Wesson .38 in. revolver for me, .303 in. Lee-Enfield rifle with fifty rounds for each of the others, hand grenades primed with four-second detonators, and pangas – machetes – for all. Purifying tablets were dropped into freshly-filled water bottles, 'Skat' anti-mosquito lotion issued. As the only white man in the party I had no wish to stand out and therefore removed my rank badges and covered my face and hands with a sooty-textured black cream reputedly created for the purpose by Elizabeth Arden. By all accounts this disguise quite upset the enemy, who assumed that by first knocking out the Europeans they would dishearten the African soldiers. In fact, I was pretty sure that such unsportsmanlike behaviour would make my askari friends very cross indeed, with dire results for any Japanese who tried it on.

Off we trudged, south along the narrow, muddy jungle track, each of us carrying our own haversack-load of thoughts. Such as, no doubt, 'If I agree to marry Manya, how many cows will her father demand as bride-price?'; 'I wonder whether I'll find my bibi's had half-a-dozen totos when I get home after these years away?'; 'I shall buy three wives with my gratuity after the war'; and even, 'Better watch out – the Jampans are about!' We kept up a good pace, considering that it was now several days since we had encountered the Japanese and they could open fire on us at any moment or be minding their own business miles away, for that matter, and if anybody was going to be surprised I hoped it would be them. All was quiet, not even birdsong; the Kabaw's animal kingdom must have learned to be silent spectators of the long and savage war between humans.

Only once was the silence broken as the patrol penetrated deeper into this no man's land. At first a distant drone then an increasing roar as a Japanese fighter, a radial-engined 'Oscar', official name Nakajima Ki-43, flashed over our heads flying south just above tree-top height. Although there was no chance that the pilot could see us we hid in the jungle to be on the safe side. This was a rare sortie by a Flying Sentai of 5 Air Division whose resources, no longer strong in Burma, had been further reduced in supporting their Army's advance on India. I was rather pleased to see this famous fighter at such close quarters without being strafed or bombed. Almost 5 miles out we came across a succession of slender sticks stuck in the ground at 10-yard intervals beside the track, each with a smallish piece of white paper in a cleft cut in the top. The penny didn't drop, and we continued on our way leaving them undisturbed. It was not until the next day that I realised their significance: they were there as markers for the benefit of Japanese night patrols and jitter-parties returning to their own positions so that 'friendly troops' warnings could be called to sentries. I wished I'd known that when it mattered most, for the sticks would have warned us of imminent trouble ahead. Still, lesson learned.

The hill feature, named on the map as Panma Taung, 1,161 feet above sea level, and the highest for miles around, was invisible to us because of the dense jungle we were moving through but we were now close to it. I decided to leave the track and assess the situation. As we whispered together Private Juma nudged me, pointing to a footprint in the mud beside a narrow stream. It had been made by a tabi, a type of lightweight footwear regarded by the Japanese as de rigueur for stealthy movement and therefore favoured for patrols and night actions. Tabi are strongly made of thick, black rubber with tough uppers of black cloth. The big toe is in a separate compartment from the other four, giving the tabi a very distinctive appearance. It was amazing good luck that we should have come off the track at the point where we did and found those prints warning that the enemy were very close at hand. Searching around, we found numerous sets of tabi-prints pointing north, whence we had come, and the askaris assured me that they were fresh, a few hours old at most. I believed them. Although few East African tribes are familiar with the jungle, belonging more to the open spaces – the plains and the hills and the desert regions – their acute powers of observation seem to make them equally good trackers in the jungle as elsewhere. I knew this from personal experience for their skill had been a bacon-saver on earlier patrols. Once again I thanked my lucky stars that I was serving with these Tanganyikan soldiers and not with British troops who could not be expected to 'read' signs in the same way. It might be that there was now an enemy patrol – or, worse, a larger force – between us and our own positions, that while we had been walking along the track they had kept to the jungle and passed within a little distance of us, heading in the opposite direction. This was an unpleasant possibility which I made myself put out of my mind for consideration later.

We resumed the track, now walking with extreme caution and straining to catch the slightest sound. We knew that we might be attacked at any moment, ambushed even, and this brought our senses to the highest pitch. I had absolute confidence in the askaris and was certain they would keep their heads and remember their training if we suddenly came upon the enemy; for my part, I must do my utmost to justify their faith in me as their officer. To the left the jungle was as thick as ever but over on the right it was becoming less dense and paddy-fields several hundred yards in width and length could be glimpsed from time to time through the trees. Not a soul was to be seen working in the paddy but the villagers might have abandoned it until they could return to grow their rice without risk of being caught in crossfire or shot as spies.

The track was somewhat drier in this area because the sun, although weak and occasional, could shine on it, and we kept to the soggiest parts to avoid boot-noise. Up in front was the leading scout, Private Rajabu, trustworthy and vigilant. Ten yards behind him was Private Mohammed, then myself as No. 3, my favourite position as it gave me control of events. Sergeant Makinde was next, followed by the others in single file at 5-yard intervals. The 'Arse-End Charlie' kept a lookout behind us and the man in front of him had his eyes skinned for any Japanese high in the trees ready to drop grenades on us, which apart from any damage they might do to the patrol would also give warning of our presence. In a minute or two I planned to swing left off the track into the thick jungle to skirt the base of the hill before climbing to the top. That way I hoped we would have a better chance of avoiding any Japanese who might be occupying it with positions dug into the front face of the lower slopes. It was also possible that there was an observation post sited high on the hill to direct the fire of 75 mm field guns. I began to suspect that Panma Taung could be crawling with Japanese.

As the patrol entered a somewhat more open area than we had yet come across, and the two scouts began cautiously to walk up a gentle incline, Private Rajabu made the 'down' hand-signal and we all melted into grass as high as an elephant's eye. Out in the open, standing in the centre of the track and only a little more than a cricket-pitch length away, was a Japanese sentry, his rifle slung over one shoulder as he gazed across the paddy fields to his left. He must at that vital moment have stepped into view. I could see Rajabu and Mohammed staring at me and signalled them to rejoin as the rest of the patrol closed up and prepared for action. Things were not going the way I had wanted and I was very much put out by this latest turn of events.

Our arrival on the scene coincided with muffled noises which seemed to be coming from the paddy-field side of the track. Voices, a single brief shouted order, the occasional ring of axes on trees, suggested the general bustle of building bunkers and digging slit trenches and octopus traps – one-man foxholes which were a speciality of the Japanese infantry. It seemed extraordinary that only one sentry appeared to have been posted, but perhaps we had bypassed an enemy listening-post, which might add to any problems in getting back home the way we had come. I decided to lie up for a while, and pondered the chances of silently snatching the sentry and bundling him away as a prisoner. It would have been quite a coup, and I was tempted to give it a try. Regretfully, I concluded that although the snatch might be accomplished our withdrawal, probably under fire and with a struggling victim, would be far too slow for comfort and we were a long way from home.

One thing was plain to see: the sentry was wearing a clean

uniform – clean, that is, by jungle campaign standards. This was most unusual and therefore of great potential significance. He seemed tall, compared with most of his kind, and well-fed; and he was not well-trained – if standing in the centre of the track instead of concealing himself in the undergrowth beside it was anything to go by. I was grateful that his lack of jungle-craft had prevented us from walking slap into the enemy camp; just a few more yards and I reckoned we should have been goners. But then, I've always been lucky. I took my hat off to the Japanese officer who had chosen to dig in here. His position was at the top of the incline with a clear forward field of fire along the track. On his left was the expanse of paddy – about 800 yards wide – so that any movement could be spotted from his camouflaged bunkers on the edge of the jungle. What he had not reckoned on was one of his men carelessly giving the game away to an inquisitive little patrol.

While we watched, crouching in the grass beside the track, I had to decide whether it was more important to carry out my orders to check on Panma Taung, in which case I should silently extricate the patrol, or try to gain an estimate of the Japanese strength. That clean uniform and the sound of axes added up to vital information that must be got back at all costs – and quickly – to our company commander. I was convinced that these were fresh troops brought up to halt the British advance while at the same time giving their comrades, the last forlorn stragglers defeated at the great battles of Imphal and Kohima, a final chance to struggle to the Chindwin River and temporary safety across on the other side. There seemed to be a sizeable number of them toiling away. The question was: How many of them? It was our duty to find out. The next question therefore had to be: How best to do so?

That we were in an awkward situation was clear enough to us all. We were on the very edge of the enemy position, almost inside it in fact, and a good 5 miles separated us from our forward troops. As to respective strengths, we knew our seven must be outnumbered; odds of two to one against us would be tricky, greater than that grossly unfair. On the credit side, for the moment at least we held the advantage of surprise, a vital card to be played for all it was worth. There seemed to be no alternative but to change our role from a 'see but do not be seen' reconnaissance to that of a patrol prepared to fight for the information it needed.

With a chinagraph pencil I wrote a brief message on the mica covering of my map and marked our precise location. Beckoning Private Mohammed to my side I whispered that he was to make his way with all speed back to camp and hand the mapcase to the Bwana Major. I added that I would allow him 15 minutes' start and he slipped away on his long, lone journey. Rather him than me, I thought. In all our minds was the strong possibility of the Japanese operating between us and our forward troops but it was a risk that had to be taken. If Mohammed were killed or captured the map would tell the enemy only what they knew well enough: the location of their own position. If we heard gunfire behind us it would warn that we must take a different route home, on a compass bearing through the jungle.

Time passed slowly once brave Mohammed had left. By now we had been watching and listening for almost 30 minutes and there were another 15 to go before I could 'light the blue touchpaper' and retire. Would our extraordinary luck hold that long, I wondered? I had decided there was only one way of judging the Japanese strength: the sentry must be shot in order to provoke a response. I studied him carefully, noting the fit of his light sandy tunic with its Private First Class rank badges, his baggy trousers with puttees up to the knee, peaked field cap with five-pointed star. His long rifle was the standard issue 6.5 mm Type 38 with 20-inch bayonet fixed. As for his thoughts, I guessed they, like those of all sentries on boring duty, were back home as he idly paced about the track.

Meanwhile the construction noises continued and another uncomfortable thought occurred to me: at any moment a working-party might be sent along the track towards us, perhaps to forage or draw water from a stream. At least we would have that huge advantage of surprise, and our firepower should be enough to stop them for a minute or two while we withdrew. We could only hope that we, the stalkers, were not ourselves being stalked from the flank or rear, to be caught in a nasty trap. And what if an enemy patrol was even now returning from a reconnaissance mission?

The askaris were superb, calm and confident and ready for anything. I couldn't be in better company. As my watch hands showed me that Private Mohammed must by now be a mile away or dead – the jungle can muffle or magnify the sound of gunfire in the most extraordinary ways – I signalled to the others that I would kill the sentry and we would wait to see the reaction. Safety-catch off, slowly raise the Sten to the shoulder, careful aim, squeeze the trigger to loose off half a magazine. I had decided that this would be more dramatic, more unnerving, than a single, deadly rifle-shot. The hail of 9 mm hitting home spun him around before he began to fall in slow motion. A little cloud of dust rose as bullets raked him from head to foot. At my signal the askaris fired 'five rounds rapid' to give the impression that a sizeable attack was going in.

It was not difficult to picture the Japanese' reaction as the Sten's roar shattered the peaceful scene, followed by our fusillade of rifle fire. An instant of terror and shocked paralysis, then a mad, wild-eyed rush to grab weapons and throw on equipment. Their comrade lying dead. Everybody off-balance. Was an attack coming in – defend from bunkers and trenches? Launch a counter-attack to protect the position from being overrun? All the fears that flash through a soldier's mind before training and discipline take over and control him. The deafening silence that followed seemed to go on forever. Then shouted commands, followed by more silence. We waited, keyed-up, knowing that in defending their position they would react aggressively. A minute or two passed. Sergeant Makinde pointed to the left. Through a gap in the vegetation we counted nine Japanese in single file working to get behind us. Over on the paddy-field side another file of similar strength led by an officer, long sword glinting silvery in his right hand and pistol in his left, was moving quickly to act as the second claw of a pincer. It was time to leave, and I signalled the patrol to run back along the track. We had kept observation for 45 minutes – it seemed much, much longer – and now had all the information we needed. I reckoned that if the enemy could respond so quickly with about twenty men ready for action there would be at least double that number left to man the unfinished defences. It was clear that we would have to fight our way out. Suddenly the prospect of a safe return seemed less than certain and I was glad I had sent Mohammed away with the map.

We hadn't covered more than about 20 yards when a burning, searing pain between my legs made me forget all about the Japanese. It was as though I was in flames. What the cause was I could not imagine but it was impossible to run another step. Shouting to the askaris to keep up rifle-fire and each man to throw one hand grenade I ripped open my fly-buttons and poured the contents of my water bottle over my burning genitals. Relief! 'Run! Run!' I roared in Swahili. Within seconds, though, the all-consuming agony was as intense as before and again I had to stop. This time I lay down on the track while two soldiers at a time emptied their bottles over my half-naked person and the others fired on the advancing Japanese. The utter absurdity of the situation had us laughing our heads off – even me, despite the mystifying pain – and I hoped that between us we had finally put out the fire. The astonished askaris could hardly have thought my antics to be white man's magic to ward off Kingi Georgie's enemies but they took it all in their stride and asked no questions. No doubt about it, though, when – if – we got back safely the entire unit would know the story before evening 'Stand To'. Nor would the story lose anything in the telling, if I knew my askaris.

For a third time we began our withdrawal. From the enemy shooting it seemed that the Japanese on the paddy-field side, where the going was easier for them, might be getting behind us. No good – I was in flames again! This time all five askaris gave covering fire while I lay in a stream, firing away with my Sten, and let the water soak me until the pain finally disappeared. It was then that I realised the cause: the screwtop on my bottle of 'Skat' lotion had worked loose, allowing the entire contents slowly to leak from my hip pocket to find the natural channel between my legs. The leaking had continued so that each time I stopped only a little was washed away; it was not until I clambered out of the stream that the bottle was empty. 'Skat', I had discovered, although lightly astringent when applied to the face and arms, had properties almost akin to phosphorous exposed to air when in contact with one's most precious and sensitive parts. I could only hope that no permanent, embarrassing damage had been done but with the Japanese closing in this was no time for intimate self-examination.

Re-formed, and the askaris now with straight faces, we kept up deterrent fire as we made our way warily back along the track, stop, listen, look, go. When I was satisfied that the stirred-up enemy seemed to have given up the pursuit we extended to 10 yards between each man, anticipating that we might walk into an ambush at any moment; with plenty of space separating us some might escape into the friendly jungle and live to tell the tale. In these circumstances 5 miles is a very long way. To increase our chances we entered the jungle from time to time in order to loop around the track before rejoining it further along. I wondered what the Japanese would have done if they had charged in, back there, and found me, black-faced, with men pouring water over my white vital statistics. At the very least they would have been surprised. A relieved Private Mohammed was the first to greet us as we passed through our defensive perimeter. He had heard our little battle raging but his own return had been uneventful, an indication that the Japanese may not yet be too close at hand in daytime. The tabi prints we had spotted had almost certainly been made by a night patrol on its way to reconnoitre our position and we must expect aggressive activity from now on.

The following morning I went off to Panma Taung to carry out yesterday's orders. This time, though, I led a strong fighting patrol of forty men and was glad of their company. Just before we left the perimeter Tomasi, grinning all over his cicatriced face, told me I had a new name. Henceforth I would be known – behind my back, of course – as 'Bwana Moto Sana'. I decided I could go along with that: 'Mister Very Hot' was the stuff of which legends are born.

The Battle

ON LEAVE IN TOKYO Major Ide of 214 Infantry Regiment was called urgently to the War Office and given his orders. He was to return at once to the Kabaw Valley on the Burma Front to lead a 'defence-and-delay' force composed mainly of 500 conscript reservists, men who had been released following service in Malaya, Singapore, and Indonesia and now recalled to duty. The force would include some who were to join or rejoin 214 Regiment and others who had been discharged 'fit for duty' from military hospitals. One of their number was Sergeant-Major Uchiyama, a veteran of the attack on Singapore and its surrender on 15 February 1942.

Ide's was one of three regiments in 33 Division: 213, 214, and 215, recruited in the Wakamatsu area and known as the 'White Tigers'. They took this name from the 17-year-old sons of Samurai forced by Imperial troops to retreat into the castle of Wakamatsu during disturbances in 1868. Twenty of these boys committed suicide when they believed the castle had fallen and had passed into legend as an inspiring example of heroic self-sacrifice. The 'White Tigers' Division had fought from the first in Burma, helping to drive the British out of the country following the 1942 invasion and two years later spearheaded their Army's advance to the very gates of India, only to be defeated at Imphal and Kohima and forced to retreat.

Was it on a sudden impulse that Sergeant-Major Uchiyama decided to pack his personal trophy of war, the large Union flag he had captured so proudly at Singapore? He remembered how he had put a burst of machine-gun fire through the flag flying over a government building before hauling it down and painting in black over the red cross, 'Commemorating the Fall of Singapore February 15 1942 Sergeant-Major Uchiyama'. Now he would take it with him to Burma to 'double' as a symbol of the defeated British and a light, woollen blanket to keep him warm at night.

It was a measure of the importance of Major Ide's task that battle-hardened veterans had been recalled to the Colours to help delay our advance. Japan's elite infantry regiments had earned their reputation as 'the best jungle fighters in the world' – and in the Kabaw they had almost three years head-start on the KAR. With no experience of warfare in the Burma jungle we were having to rely on our year's hard training in Ceylon, but we had already found to our cost that there is no substitute for the real thing. British military strategists were convinced that once the monsoon ended in October the Japanese would stand and fight at the foot of the Kabaw Valley with their backs to the Chindwin River in order to gain time for their forces to regroup and establish defensive positions in depth. Over the past weeks we had made sporadic contact with the enemy and 14 Army needed a stream of reliable information on which to base Operation Capital, the drive on Rangoon and the retaking of the whole of Burma. Passed down, down, down the chain of command until it could go no lower came the order from on high: 'Find out where General Tanaka Nabuo intends to stand and fight.' This could be done only by intensive patrolling, a high-risk duty which fell to the infantry platoon commander.

The strategists were about to be proved correct. Major Ide and his force arrived at Kalewa on the Chindwin in the middle of September and left Kalemyo at the southern end of the Kabaw on the 28th to begin an operation which would prove to be little more than a suicide mission. Ide's orders were to advance north towards us along the main track, as close as he could get to a large village named Yazagyo, building a succession of bunker positions – mini-fortresses – as he did so. He would occupy the one closest to us and issue forth to attack; only when the pressure of our advance became irresistible would he retire to the next of his prepared positions and repeat the process.

The Intelligence Section and I were now attached temporarily to the leading company of the Ugandans' battalion. The previous day my reconnaissance patrol to find out whether the Japanese were occupying Panma Taung Hill would, but for the alertness of Private Rajabu, have walked into a strong enemy force busily constructing defensive bunkers. Today I was to complete the mission to Panma Taung, leading a strong fighting patrol of the 'I' Section and a Uganda platoon with its commander, Lieutenant Macdonald. We made our way along the track by sections in extended order, ready for anything and anticipating an ambush at any moment, but so far there was no sign of the enemy. Two miles further on we left the track remembering that the Japanese, too, preferred moving through the jungle and we might therefore meet head-on or pass one another unseen going in opposite directions. It was better not to dwell on such possibilities but concentrate on the job in hand. With the knowledge gained yesterday that the enemy were now dug-in in bunkers and octopus traps straddling the track Macdonald and I decided to make a wide half-circle around their positions and climb the hill from its rear. It was unlikely that they would have established listening-posts so far out on the flank but we might find a strong body settled-in on the hill and were ready to fight for the information we needed. If things worked out for us we would return home by a different route from the way we had come.

The plan of action worked well and we began to walk warily up Panma Taung's jungle-covered lower slopes. Suddenly the leading scout, Private Wambunyu, the sole Kikuyu in the 'I' Section, made the 'down' hand-signal and ducked into the undergrowth, the rest of us following suit. In a clearing ahead there was a small group of open-sided bashas, grass huts, which could be an enemy camp. We laid up and watched and listened for any movement or sound but nothing stirred and all was quiet. All the same, I didn't like the look of the bashas. Deciding that they must be investigated I led the section for a closer look while the platoon took up concealed defensive positions. Twenty yards or so from the three bashas set close together I signalled Sergeant Makinde and Private Lugembe to go forward while I and the rest of the section crouched in the tall grass covering them and ready to open fire at the first sign or sound of trouble. Making skilful use of the trees and vegetation for protection and concealment the two men crept up to the nearest basha and looked over its low, thatched-grass walls – barely waist-high – before stealing across to the second one. It, too, must have been empty.

We watched as Makinde entered the third basha while Lugembe remained outside, vigilant, rifle at the ready, peering into the jungle beyond. Makinde hand-signalled us to join him. We found him looking down at a wounded Japanese soldier lying on a 'do-it-yourself' bed, the kind that any jungle-trained soldier can knock up in a few minutes. (Method: cut six short, vee-notched stakes from saplings. Sharpen these to a point at one end and push into the soft earth to form the bed's outline shape. Next, lay two straight, strong sapling-lengths into the six notches to complete the parallel sides. Using creeper, lash a couple of dozen thinner sticks across the two sides as the base on which to lay your grass 'mattress'. Sleep easy 9 inches above the ground.)

The enemy soldier lay motionless on his back, his eyes wide as he gazed up at us surrounding the bed. He was fully-dressed but the right leg of his sandy-khaki trousers had been cut away from the groin to the knee to allow a wide field dressing to be wrapped around his thigh. The bandage was heavily blood-stained. He was young, perhaps 20, with sparse black stubble around the sides of his chin, none at the point. His field service cap lay on the ground beside him. Although I must have looked to him identical to the askaris – my face and hands were completely blackened and I wore no rank badges – he turned his head towards me as I stood at his side. Our eyes met. Could he have wondered at a black man with blue eyes? But then, almost certainly he would never before have seen Africans in the flesh. He seemed to give a slight smile – was he bravely concealing an inner terror at the sight of these huge, black men looming over him? I guessed he was a casualty of yesterday's fierce little action fought as I withdrew my reconnaissance patrol with that damned 'Skat' lotion searing my genitals.

I whispered to Private Juma to give him a drink. Juma took his water bottle from his belt and unscrewed the top before passing the bottle to the Japanese. He put it to his lips and gulped greedily. With no word from me an askari fumbled into a pocket and took out a biscuit and handed it to the wounded man. We watched in silence as he took a bite from it. He was hungry, but chewing was clearly difficult for him. Crumbs framed his lips and stayed there. What were we to do with him? The major's orders were explicit and unequivocal: Panma Taung, of tactical importance to both British and Japanese and shown on the map as a Survey triangulation point must be checked-out thoroughly. Yesterday I had used my initiative when instead of recce-ing the hill I had chosen to attack the Japanese to try to estimate their strength but today nothing must prevent us from carrying out our orders to the letter.

Quickly I weighed up the factors, making what in military terms is called 'an appreciation of the situation', thus: The Japanese are in the immediate vicinity, and in strength. We are behind their known positions. At any moment an enemy force – a small recce patrol or a strong fighting patrol like ours – may come our way, perhaps returning to the bashas as their hill-base; they would not have deserted their wounded comrade. We must not loiter around bashas set in the open and built and occupied by the enemy. Moreover, they may be booby-trapped, probably protected also with trip-wires hung with cans containing loose pebbles to rattle as warning of an unfriendly approach. In jungle-warfare, particularly, where visibility is so often measured in yards, silence is golden, just as one hopes 'the other side' will make noises – talking, moving clumsily through the vegetation – which give away their move-ments and position. In the stagnant air the smell of cigarettes smoked hours earlier tells heightened senses of a patrol's pas-sage. Yesterday, lying-up in the long, trackside grass watching, noting, listening, I had contemplated snatching the unwary sentry but decided our six-man patrol was too weak and too far from home to have a sporting chance of success. Now, today, we had strength enough but were only halfway into our mission and must not be hampered by a wounded prisoner.

The 'courses open' narrowed. Clearly, we could not take the man with us, carrying him as we explored the hill. Nor should I detach any men to take him back as prisoner to our perimeter miles away: it would be madness to divide and weaken our small force. Conclusion: My orders and the patrol's safety must be paramount. The wounded man must not be allowed to remain where he was, to tell his comrades of black troops roaming the hill. Therefore he must die. But the sound of a revolver-shot would bring the Japanese to the attack. Therefore what must be done must be done silently.

Before leaving our perimeter I had ordered bayonets to be fixed, ready against ambush or other nasty surprise. I whispered again to Private Juma. He raised his rifle and with the point of the bayonet gently drew the wounded man's tunic to one side, exposing an inch or two of bare, hairless chest. The soldier's arms bent back, palms of his hands upward as if in unintended horizontal surrender as the cold steel began its slow downward thrust into his heart. His eyes locked into mine and pierced my soul.

★ ★ ★

I was glad to return to 36 KAR for the battalion was again leading the advance and fighting hard against the defence-and-delay force. Our patrols went out every day in search of the enemy who were themselves patrolling aggressively and casualties mounted on both sides. Company Sergeant-Major O'Hara had been shot and killed by a Japanese officer feigning death. The same day Lieutenant Britton was killed in a skirmish while out on patrol only two days after joining the battalion. Malign Fate had pointed her finger at him, for he ought not to have been with us at all. On his arrival at the Front from Ceylon he had been posted to a Uganda battalion, only at once to be ordered to join 36 KAR to replace an officer evacuated suffering from deep shock following an ambush.

Next to go were Major Firth, commanding my old 'D' Company from Somaliland days, Company Sergeant-Major Birtwistle and Sergeant Brown of the Mortar Platoon. A patrol from the company ran into a strong party of Japanese advancing with the bayonet and Firth went forward in order to bring down mortar fire while his Company attacked in strength. The enemy positions were successfully overrun but a machine-gun counter-attack was launched from others which were concealed. In the withdrawal the three men were reported missing and it was not until the following day that the bodies of two of them – Firth and Brown – were found. The head of one had been cut off by a sword. Of Birtwistle there was no sign and it was not until months later that he was reported to have died in Rangoon Gaol as a prisoner-of-war, where our 'missing' askaris might also be held. There was a strong belief that Firth may have given his life to save Birtwistle, who was seen to fall as though wounded, by staying with him until the Japanese burst on to them, killing Firth and Brown but sparing Birtwistle. Those of us who knew Firth would expect such courageous self-sacrifice. Among the African dead and missing was my friend from 16 Platoon in Somaliland, brave Lance-Corporal Shuli, the ever-cheerful Wanyamwezi Bren-gunner whose slight build concealed physical strength and amazing endurance in carrying his heavy weapon hour after hour on route marches and training exercises.

The patrol sent out to search for the missing men ran into the enemy and fought hard, but Captain Dawson was killed in the action. Like Britton, Dawson was the newest of newcomers to the battalion. Most of his service since his arrival in East Africa in 1942 had been with second-line battalions guarding Italians in prisoner-of-war camps near the Ngong Hills out on the Athi Plains. Desperate to escape from the endless drudgery of this depressing duty he had applied for any and every training course that became available but it was not until two years later that he succeeded in being posted to Ceylon, then Burma. He had been with us barely a week. Searching a pack lying beside the body of an enemy soldier killed in the action I found a large Union Jack with Japanese characters in black paint over the St George's Cross. Sergeant-Major Uchiyama would not be going home to Japan; and a much-travelled flag was back at last in British hands.

A day or two later Lieutenant Murray was killed. He had been to brigade headquarters and was returning to the battalion with orders when his driver mistakenly drove beyond our foremost defences and towards the enemy positions. Jumping from the Jeep Murray bravely engaged the advancing Japanese with his revolver while the driver struggled unavailingly to turn the Jeep around in a hail of fire. There could be only one outcome: both men were killed. They would have been wiser to abandon the Jeep at once and dash into the welcoming cover of the jungle. That way they would have had a sporting chance of escaping.

Despite our losses morale remained high, but the feeling began to grow that the pressure to push on with all speed down the valley was resulting in insufficient reconnaissance, which in turn led to casualties that might have been avoided. In an attempt to reduce the casualty rate among Europeans the commanding officer ordered that patrols were to be led by African sergeants. No matter how militarily well-intentioned, his order could have been interpreted in the battalion as a readiness to conserve European officers' and NCOs' lives at the expense of African ones. A way was found of appearing to obey the order without doing so: patrols left the perimeter under command of African sergeants and were at once joined by officers or British NCOs.

The Japanese had suffered heavy casualties since their arrival in the Kabaw at the beginning of October. Major Ide's second-in-command, Captain Osawa, who was to have joined 214 Infantry Regiment as commander of No. 1 Battalion, was wounded at Kangyi, 8 miles south of Yazagyo, and evacuated. Osawa's place was taken by another officer, Captain Sakae Katagiri, with orders to force-march north with forty or so men and machine-guns along the track towards Yazagyo in order to block our continuing advance. The two antagonists,

36 KAR and 214 Regiment, closed on one another and the scene was set for 'the battle near Indainggyi'.

Our patrols found the enemy occupying a low hill feature, code-named 'Moshi', and dug-in on its two 'pimples' close to the main track. The colonel had for many months, even before we left Ceylon, been showing unmistakable signs of strain, and these had grown worse in the past weeks. With great moral courage, fully recognising the serious disciplinary risk that as a subordinate he was running by his action, the adjutant, Captain Sinclair, decided he must press the colonel most strongly – for his own sake but particularly the battalion's – to report sick and be evacuated. On the brink of total nervous collapse – to which he succumbed the following day – the colonel accepted Sinclair's urgings supported by the medical officer and was replaced at once by Lieutenant-Colonel Robson of the Royal Scots, a Regular officer who had served with the KAR in the Abyssinian and Madasgascar campaigns. Now the pressure to advance was transferred to Robson, who decided to launch an immediate, full-scale attack on 'Moshi'.

Preparations for the assault began early the next morning, 3 November, with companies moving to tactical positions and strong reconnaissance groups and fighting patrols sent out to gain latest information. The Japanese would have known from the previous day's low-level aerial photo-reconnaissance Hurricane and our probing activity on the ground that they must expect a heavy attack within hours and made their plans to meet it. Delays of one kind and another postponed the attack and it was not until 1703 hours that the assault was launched; this was dangerously late if things did not go exactly according to plan, which in battle they rarely do. The risk was that there might be no time before dusk to dig-in once the pimples were taken and repulse enemy counter-attacks. Had the pressure on the colonel from above not been so strong he should have waited until the next morning, when the battle might have had a different outcome.

Tanks opened up with harassing fire from their machine-guns and 2-pounders, and 3.7-in. howitzers and 25-pounders bombarded 'Moshi' for five minutes to zero hour, when Major Gash's company attacked one of the two pimples and Onslow's 'C' Company the other. In the fighting that followed, 'C' Company succeeded in capturing their objective only to be driven off it by heavy fire from medium machine-guns in concealed positions; and Gash's troops were mown down by machine-gun fire in their brave charge up the lightly-covered slope to the enemy trenches and forced to withdraw. We could not bring in the wounded, nor recover the dead, and could only hope that our wounded would not be killed where they lay. Our casualties were grievous: one officer and one British warrant officer killed, and one officer missing; Major Onslow, shot in the head, losing an eye; eleven askaris killed and two missing; and sixteen wounded. The enemy held tenaciously on to the pimples and we moved back 200 yards along the track to form a defensive box and prepare another plan to dislodge them.

More patrols went out in search of the enemy during the next few days, snipers spent hours in the jungle patiently waiting for a target, standing patrols and listening posts took up position night and day beside tracks which the Japanese used. Air strikes were called to our aid, the Royal Air Force visual control officer attached to us radioing for 'cab ranks' of Hurricanes to bomb and strafe the Japanese positions marked for them with mortar smoke bombs. For their part, the Japanese sent their 'Oscar' fighters – as many as ten at a time – to shoot down supply-dropping Dakotas and make strafing runs on our trackside positions, attacking with cannon and machine-guns as they roared overhead just above tree-top height.

Every night, well after midnight, the Japanese staged jitter-parties whose purpose was to lower our morale and encourage us to fire into the blackness and give away our positions with rifle flashes whilst at the same time wasting quantities of ammunition. The technique rarely varied. First, there would be an attempt to slither unseen and unheard into the 'box', passing between slit-trenches before throwing hand grenades into our midst. If our vigilance prevented them getting in amongst us, there would come the unmistakable sound of grenades being struck on their base, necessary to detonate the fuse before they were hurled at us. This activity was accompanied by throwing stones and taunting us in English – 'Johnny, here I am!' and 'Johnny, we're coming to kill you!' – to encourage wild shooting by rattled askaris.

One night Private Antoni of the Signals Platoon slept in his slit-trench when he should have been fully alert and allowed Japanese to worm their way into the battalion headquarters position before being killed. For this most serious crime, which ranks with showing cowardice, desertion in the face of the enemy, and casting away arms in the face of the enemy, whose penalty is death by firing squad, Private Antoni was brought before the commanding officer after the dawn 'Stand To' and morning meal. The CO's 'Orderly Room' was necessarily held al fresco amongst the trenches. The colonel stood with the adjutant, Regimental Sergeant-Major Wilkinson, the African Regimental Sergeant-Major and the Signals Platoon commander as Private Antoni and his escort were ordered to attention. As a headquarters officer with nowhere else to be at the time, I stood, by chance, a couple of yards from the group while the colonel heard the case.

There was no doubt of Private Antoni's guilt; the problem was to award a punishment which reflected the gravity of the offence while not taking the accused and witnesses away from the battalion for a court-martial while we were fighting the enemy. The colonel announced his decision: twelve lashes of the kiboko. Antoni was lucky to be spared the firing squad. It was more than two years since that unforgettable flogging at Mandera in British Somaliland, when I had found Private Sumani asleep in his sentry-box inside the Italian prisoner-of-war camp, and I had hoped never to witness one again. The moment Antoni heard his sentence he broke away from his escort and ran to a nearby slit trench where his rifle and equipment lay. In an instant he had drawn a hand grenade from a pouch and pulled out the pin, clasping the springlever tight to the side of the grenade so that the fuse could not be detonated. Taking two or three paces towards us, he drew his right arm back in the throwing position. We froze. At that range none of us could hope to survive the blasting fragmentation of a Mills grenade with its four-second fuse. The colonel, in a quiet voice coming from the corner of his mouth as he stared at Antoni, ordered me, 'John, shoot him'.

I dropped down beside a trench and picked up a rifle. Nobody else moved. I could see troops staring at the scene; they, too, were transfixed. It must have made an extraordinary tableau. On one knee, I raised the rifle to the 'aim' and with a quick bolt-action loaded a round into the breech. For long seconds the stand-off continued, Antoni poised to throw the grenade, I with my rifle ready to shoot. But this was no cowboy 'Western', it was a real-life, high-stakes drama being acted out on the battlefield. I was thinking fast: if I shot Antoni dead the grenade must consign us all to kingdom come, probably him included, as it fell from his hand and the lever sprang up. I decided I must take a last-chance gamble rather than kill one of our own men only to get ourselves blown to smithereens seconds later. Aiming an inch or two off from his left thigh I fired, reloading at once, hoping that my deliberate near-miss would bring him to his senses. Instead, with a wild, desperate look on his face he very, very slowly took another pace towards us until now we were only 5 or 6 yards apart. I aimed above his left knee, squeezed the trigger and fired. With a scream of agony as his femur shattered Antoni fell to the ground before dragging himself to a trench where he lay moaning, the grenade still grasped tight in his right hand. Bravely, an askari prised his hand open and made the grenade safe before Antoni was hauled out and carried away to the Regimental Aid Post.

As though nothing untoward had happened the imperturbable Sinclair shouted something as banal as 'Shauri nakwisha'- 'the affair's finished' – and the drama was over. A rumour soon reached me that some of Private Antoni's fellow-tribesmen were threatening to kill me in revenge. I did not need telling how easy it would be to shoot me in the back while out on patrol but I was sure the threat was an idle one made by a few hotheads and paid it no attention.

That night, as I peered out of my slit-trench waiting for the regular Japanese jitter-party to begin, I sipped my hoarded eight-fluid-ounce rum ration and thought over the morning's events. (Delivery of the rum was irregular, to say the least, and when it arrived one had to decide whether to drink it all in a single, glorious 'go', or spread the enjoyment over four days, or even save it to celebrate a worst moment survived. Then again, should it be diluted with water, or sipped neat? I plumped for a binge.) Here you are, I told myself as a wonderful warm glow enveloped me, within a stone's throw of a fanatically-brave enemy whose one aim in life is to kill you, and one of your own men decides to try to do it for them. Funny, in a way.

Later that month Private Devesias Ndembo of 13 (Nyasaland) Battalion succeeded where Private Antoni might be said to have failed. Brought before his company commander on a disciplinary charge, found guilty, and awarded an appropriate punishment, he plotted his revenge. That night he crept to the lighted company headquarters mess-tent and lobbed a hand grenade in among his officers and senior British NCOs with devastating results: unable to escape before the grenade exploded, one officer was killed and four officers and a warrant officer were seriously wounded. Ndembo was tried by court-martial and shot by firing squad.

★ ★ ★

It was one of war's ironies that Sinclair should go through the Kabaw Valley campaign without a scratch only to fall victim to a Type 78 grenade while conducting a training exercise in India. The Type 78 is a fearsome weapon of war. It is about the size of a small thermos flask and, like the thermos, its top screws off. It contains a noxious substance, white phosphorous, which every schoolchild knows ignites on exposure to air. All phosphorous needs is a little oxygen – and off it goes, emitting dense clouds of white smoke and burning away until it exhausts itself. There is only one way to stop it: immerse it in water. For some obscure reason the phosphorous grenade is not regarded as coming within the chemical warfare category and, like napalm, can be used legitimately and without restriction. Its uses are in close contact with the enemy to smoke out bunkers or deep trenches and foxholes: pop one through a bunker loophole and the occupants will either appear in double-quick time or they will die inside in a particularly horrible fashion.

The Type 78 is simple to activate. Screw off the top and a roll of white tape with a lead weight is revealed. Place the thumb of your right hand firmly on the lead weight, then swing back your right arm and throw the grenade at the target, releasing the thumb in good time as you do so. The lead weight pulls out the tape, arming the explosive charge within, which on impact with any solid matter bursts open the canister and showers sticky blobs of burning phosphorous in all directions. It goes without saying that great care is necessary in the training of troops in the use of the '78'; they must fully understand its deadly effect if they do not keep well away from its 'beaten zone'.

The heat of the Indian sun around its zenith was too great even for seasoned African soldiers and training was therefore carried out before eleven o'clock in the morning and after four o'clock in the afternoon. Briefed to take part in a battalion-scale exercise involving the use of live ammunition – mortars, machine-guns, and small arms – Sinclair, now a major – led his company out of Ranchi Camp before dawn one morning and marched 10 miles to an area remote from roads in Bihar Province's immense, dry, waterless landscape. We were learning the hard way that heat exhaustion is a killer which must be guarded against. Soldiers had died in its fatal embrace as they lay down for the mandatory ten-minute rest in every hour's marching – and left this world without a sound, not even a murmur, apparently fit one minute, dead the next. Medical knowledge of dehydration and its capacity for causing sudden death was relatively slight and only now, with tragic experience, was it being realised that the Army's route-march discipline forbidding troops to drink from their water bottles except on an officer's order – an order never given at the first halt – should be replaced with generous, authorised, life-giving drinking from adequate supplies and laced with salt replacement tablets.

The signal for 36 KAR's exercise to begin was to be a burst of white smoke from a Type 78 thrown by Sinclair himself at a safe distance from his men. He screwed off the top and thumbed the lead weight, which unaccountably at once fell off and rolled away. No lead weight, no explosion – or so it should be, according to the training manual as Sinclair, a former small arms instructor, knew well. As he stooped to recover the weight his steel helmet struck his Sten gun a glancing blow, the grenade fell from his grasp and rolled across the ground, the tape rewinding as it did so. A sudden sharp explosion and the '78' burst, at once enveloping Sinclair in a cloud of furiously-burning white phosphorous which ignited his thin jungle-green uniform so that he was on fire from head to foot. His orderly and the nearest platoon commander fought to beat out the flames but water is the only antidote against phosphorous and there was none within miles. The experience of pain beyond description caused Sinclair's nervous system to cut out; probably it was deep shock that mercifully shut off his brain's function. A red Verey light fired into the sky halted the exercise as medical dressers raced to his aid and injected him with a double shot of morphine. Realising that every second counted, that his life was hanging by the slenderest of threads, askari stretcher-bearers never once paused for a breather on their headlong, 4-mile rush across rough country to a Jeep which could get him to Ranchi's field hospital.

Fortunately for Sinclair the medical officers and nurses knew exactly what to do, and had the means of doing it. Particles of phosphorous in both eyes were neutralised with copper sulphate solution and permanent damage – full or partial blindness – averted. Three- and four-degree burns covered 30 per cent of his body, his left arm, left leg and the left side of his face being most seriously affected. Shock and a consequent loss of fluid causes the kidneys to go into crisis in severe burns cases and the treatment for this is non-stop blood plasma – in Sinclair's situation, three quart-bottles every twenty-four hours for the first two weeks and four-hourly penicillin injections for the same period. To attempt to stimulate his appetite a half-bottle of champagne accompanied his high-protein evening meal. (I had learned that champagne is highly regarded in medical circles as an important stimulant, having overheard doctors and nurses urging Lieutenant Broughton to try to drink it as he lay dying in the middle of the night from scrub typhus in a Kabaw Valley field hospital.)

After weeks of intensive treatment Sinclair was put on board a a hospital train to Poona, cool and green, with its large, permanent military hospital, for a period of further treatment and convalescence before being returned to Britain in the hospital ship *Somersetshire*. During the voyage, and now able to take a few painful steps, he was about to sink gratefully into a deckchair on the Promenade Deck when a female voice rasped, 'These chairs are for staff only, not for patients.' He knew then that he was back in the real world.

Out of action and back in training in Bihar I had my own experience of the risks associated with dehydration. On that occasion the battalion was to march 20 miles to a training area, leaving Camp at 2 a.m. in Field Service Marching Order to cover the distance in the relative cool of the night before beginning a three-day, large-scale exercise. I had been decidedly unwell the day before – lightheaded and dizzy and, thanks to a severely upset stomach, I must have lost vital body fluids – and dreaded the prospect of a long, gruelling route march, let alone one in full kit: large pack, haversack, groundsheet, Sten gun, revolver, ammunition, and more besides, weighing 60 lb or so. I went to bed early hoping against hope that my symptoms would be gone before we marched out but when Private Rajabu woke me at 1 a.m. I was feeling worse, not better.

As adjutant, the colonel's staff officer, I would have responsibilities throughout the exercise that could not easily be passed at a moment's notice to another officer if I reported sick. Besides, how would it appear to others if I announced without warning that I was too ill to march? It was not an example I was prepared to set. I sensed that I was dehydrated when we set off in the stifling night-time heat and before long I was in a bad way, in a nightmare world where every step had me lurching and bumping into askaris as the seemingly endless miles slowly unwound. What kept me putting one foot in front of the other, repeating itself over and over in my whirling head, was the Army dictum: 'An officer never falls out on the line of march.' I was on the point of collapse, legs rubbery, when I had the last vestige of control to grasp that I must take on water, no matter what. Vaguely hoping that in the darkness nobody would spot me drinking in defiance of standing orders I eased my water bottle from its webbing harness and gulped half the contents. Miraculously, within minutes I felt my strength returning and my head clearing so that I was able to carry on. Surreptitious swigs kept me going and the moment we halted to make camp half a canvas chagoul of cool water inside me and the other half poured over my head, soaking me to the skin, made my recovery complete. How close had I come, I wondered, to fatal dehydration? And would a similar disobedience of orders have saved our askari who died from heat exhaustion during a march a week earlier?

Captain Rode's accident was as appalling in its consequences as Sinclair's; where the two differed was that Fate lay in wait to strike Rode a second, bizarre blow should he have the temerity to survive the first. Rode was a staff captain at brigade headquarters bivouacked 2 or 3 miles behind the Kabaw Valley front line and protected by a Defence Platoon of the kind I had commanded whilst serving my period of penance in Tanganyika and Ceylon. Japanese activity in the area ensured that a high level of alertness was maintained at all times within the perimeter. Throughout the night officers took their turn on duty. At 2 a.m. Rode was relieved and made his way through the pouring rain to the bivouac he shared with another officer. His fumbling in the darkness with the laced-up entrance woke the other occupant who instinctively reached for his revolver and fired, convinced that he was being attacked by a Japanese who had slithered through the defences. Rode took a .38 bullet full in the stomach, sustaining a massive wound that would never heal.

After the war he became an export manager with a British company which did much of its business with Nigeria. His job took him frequently to Lagos and he came to know the air route well. Flying out on his umpteenth trip and unable to sleep he looked out of his window and saw the sun rising in the south-east. Puzzled, he rang for a stewardess and pointed out the phenomenon. Or had the aircraft been diverted? He was not satisfied with her sweet smile and those anodyne words of reassurance that cabin staff are trained to give nervous passengers and at his insistence she agreed to speak to the captain. She found consternation on the flight-deck. The captain told her that the British Overseas Airways Hermes was hundreds of miles off course, fuel was running low and reserves almost exhausted, and the nearest airfield was beyond range. Soon, very soon, they would come down in the Saharan desert wastes and the cabin crew must prepare the passengers immediately for inevitable disaster. How could this have happened? As so often, human error was the cause: magnetic variation of 6 degrees from true north had accidentally been set on the gyro-compass by the navigator as 60 degrees and it was only when the sun began to rise above the horizon that the terrible shock of realisation had come to the crew.

'Mayday' messages radioed from the doomed Hermes gave its identity, approximate position, present course, the nature of the emergency, the number of souls on board, and the captain's intention to crash-land. Rescue services were alerted and prepared to send out search parties. The passengers waited for death. When the crash came it could have been far worse. The captain had opted for a wheels-up, belly landing and as the airliner smashed at high speed over the ground, leaping, grinding, lurching, shedding bits and pieces, its body mercifully maintained some degree of structural integrity so that no passengers died in the crash. The captain was only slightly hurt but the first officer died the following day from head injuries.

A first rule of survival in these circumstances is: stay with the aircraft. Perhaps for good reason the captain decided that all must walk to the nearest settlement shown on the map and off they trudged, men and women of all ages, children, babes in arms, struggling hour after hour through soft, thigh-deep sand, up and down steep dunes, across rough scrub and rock. For Rode the ordeal was worse than for many others: his shot-away stomach and bowel intestines had necessitated colostomy and the physical effort he was now called on to make, combined with ever-present pain and the Sahara's searing heat, quickly brought him to the limit of his endurance. Somehow he kept going, perhaps determined to do so because he remembered that 'an officer never falls out on the line of march'. When a French Foreign Legion rescue column found them he could not have lasted another day. He never recovered and died a few short years later, an innocent casualty both of war in the jungle and ordeal in the desert. Fate struck a second blow, also, at a woman survivor of the air crash and her baby. Pushing her pram to the shops in quiet, peaceful Lyme Regis in Dorset she and the child were smashed to death by a wheel which sheared from a heavy truck and careered down the town's steep hill.

Five Paces

THE SMALL FORCE comprising my Intelligence Section and Lieutenant Mann's platoon continued our attachment to the Ugandans' leading company. Today Mann's orders were to take his platoon south along the track to check whether the Japanese had advanced overnight to within 2 miles of our position. If the coast was clear he was to dig in on the 'friendly' side of a wide chaung and send a runner back with his report, when the Ugandans' company would move forward to join him. This was to be my rest day following a period of leading reconnaissance and fighting patrols and I waved the thirty rifles on their way as they disappeared into the jungle.

It was not much more than an hour later that I heard a strange, almost unearthly noise, something like a long, drawn-out sigh mixed incongruously with the pounding of boots. There was no sound of voices at all. I rushed to join all the others running to their defensive positions, but this was not a weird preliminary to a Japanese attack, it was the sound of Mann's askaris streaming back into the perimeter. Their eyes rolling in terror and shock almost all of them were without weapons or equipment. Once inside the perimeter they stood there, gasping for breath and all too clearly completely demoralised. The last to return minutes later was Mann himself, his black-painted face contorted in rage. 'They ran away!' he shouted. 'They ran away and left me!' The platoon had walked into an ambush, the jungle suddenly erupting into an inferno of machine-gun and rifle fire and the roar and flame and smoke of bursting hand grenades, of shouts of 'Banzai! Banzai! Banzai!' In an instant the entire platoon panicked and could think only of escape. In full view of the enemy they had turned tail, throwing down their arms and equipment, their entrenching tools, anything that might slow their headlong flight. All thirty must have run virtually non-stop to gain the safety of the perimeter.

It didn't call for much imagination to picture the scene of the ambush. But what was now to be done about the disaster? As commander of our small force I realised only too well the seriousness of the situation. The troops had run from the enemy without a single man – private, corporal, or sergeant – doing his duty. So quickly had the platoon fled that they had not fired a single shot, had suffered no casualties. Had they lost men dead, wounded, or even captured, if only just some of them had kept their nerve, there might be something to be said in their favour. In these circumstances, though, there could be no excuse. This was Mann's catastrophic baptism of fire. He had joined the battalion only a week or two earlier as a reinforcement officer fresh from jungle training in Ceylon and I blamed the commanding officer and Mann's company commander for sending an inexperienced officer with me when clearly I needed someone who, like me, had served a fair time with the battalion and knew his men. The story that the askaris had run away would be reported at once to brigade headquarters, then up to division, even to Army, no doubt embroidered the higher it travelled, so that eventually it would be rumoured that an entire company of Tanganyikans had fled, not just a single, ambushed platoon, leaving the Ugandans to clear up the mess.

Mann suddenly went from rage into a state of deep shock, unable to speak coherently so that only mumbled words came out in fits and starts. He began to stagger as his legs turned to rubber. I supported him to his bivouac and laid him down on the grass bedding, then washed the black cream from his face, talking all sorts of reassuring rubbish as I did so. One thing was clear: in no circumstances could he fight until he had fully recovered. At the same time as I was doing my best to tend him I was thinking hard: what could be done to attempt to minimise the scale of the disaster? How could the reputation of our Tanganyika battalion be restored immediately in the eyes of the Ugandans? I felt a personal responsibility for the shameful flight even though neither I nor my Intelligence Section were directly involved.

There never has been a time when soldiers have not run from the battlefield; I knew this well enough from accounts I had read of battles stretching back through the ages. The histories of famous British regiments, household names, starkly tell of panic turned to rout at the same time as they record deeds of unimaginable steadfastness against overwhelming odds. It was well known in Burma that a company of one of Britain's proudest county regiments had run from their hill position, leaving it to be recaptured at heavy cost by an Indian battalion. But to the officer who sees his men flee the disgrace must sear his very soul: he would never have conceived such a happening. It was no wonder that the ambush and his askaris' panic had thrown Mann into shock.

From my patrol reports, and now the ambush, it seemed certain that the Japanese must have completed construction of a small chain of fall-back defensive positions and were advancing up the Kabaw Valley towards us on a 'delay' offensive. The ambush point was at the very chaung that Mann had been ordered to occupy if he found it clear of the enemy. The company commander decided to launch a company-strength attack immediately. It was all too plain to me that if our battalion's honour, to say nothing of its morale, were to be retrieved – at least in part – I must insist on leading the attack with my Intelligence Section. Fortunately, for he might well have lost confidence in us, Major Willis understood and agreed. His plan was that we should enter the jungle as soon as we left our perimeter and follow minor tracks off to the east before turning west to block the main track behind the enemy position. The Intelligence Section would lead. Once contact was made I was to reconnoitre the Japanese position and report back. The subsequent company-strength attack, by infantry only and without artillery support, would be spearheaded by the section. It all sounded quite simple, and urgent preparations were made to leave in 30 minutes' time.

For weeks Tomasi had been reminding me that he was no longer a personal servant but an enlisted private soldier and, as such, had a right to accompany me on operations. Much as I sympathised with his point of view I was concerned at his lack of experience, for his training in Ceylon and here in Burma had been only basic and he was far from being a trained soldier. Each time he pleaded his case I told him that I, not he, would decide when the time had come for him to go a-fighting. Matters were not helped when he listened to his comrades' stories of our adventures on successful reconnaissance and fighting patrols and dawn attacks. There was no doubt that so far I had been lucky, and soldiers like to follow a lucky leader, but I did not need to be reminded that one's stock of good luck can run out when it is needed most. That knowledge had made it easy for me to deny Tomasi's repeated requests.

He must have decided to give me one last chance. I did not welcome his interruption for I had just finished briefing the section and was now busy preparing myself for what lay ahead. 'A good soldier always looks after his weapon', and looking after mine was a task I never allowed anybody to do for me. Methodically I stripped down my Sten gun and closely inspected every one of its component parts before cleaning and polishing them and giving the mechanism a light film of rifle-oil. When that was done to my satisfaction I pulled the barrel through with 'four by two' flannelette so that the rifled steel shone bright, and finished off by wiping and polishing every individual round of ammunition before loading five magazines. My .38-in. Smith & Wesson revolver and its ammunition came in for the same concentrated, self-preservation attention. Finally, I unscrewed the base of each of my four Mills hand grenades to check that they were fused at four seconds: this ultra-short period discouraged the enemy from picking up the grenade and throwing it back. I needed to know that the correct time-fuses were in place because grenades propelled from launchers have a higher trajectory than those thrown by hand and are fused to detonate after seven seconds.

At the best of times the Sten Mk.1, a cheap, mass-produced machine-carbine for use in close-quarter fighting, was notoriously unreliable. If the stock were unintentionally banged on the ground the safety-catch could release itself and the gun fire off half a magazine in seconds, perhaps shooting its owner in the process. And if dirt got into the firing mechanism – all too easy in the mud and filth of the jungle – it might well jam with fatal consequences for the poor devil who had had to put his faith in it. Not for the first time I bitterly regretted that order in Ceylon, issued shortly before we set out for Burma, recalling all our Thompson .45-inch calibre sub-machine guns, for the 'Tommy gun' was a well-engineered, accurate weapon with excellent stopping power. What had been tried and tested by Al Capone in Chicago in the twenties was first class, but we had been sent to fight with markedly inferior weapons against an enemy described repeatedly to us as 'the best jungle-fighters in the world'.

I heard Tomasi out, weighing up the risks as I did so. This was to be a planned attack by about a hundred men and therefore very different from a small patrol penetrating enemy territory, when every man must play his specialist, well-trained part. Yes, I told him, he could come, provided he stayed five paces behind me at all times. Not ten paces, I stressed, nor two paces, but five. And when the shooting began he must throw himself to the ground, take cover, and wait for orders. Understood? His face lit up and he rushed away to get himself ready.

With two scouts out in front I took up my usual position as No. 3, where I could keep an eye on them and control the pace and direction of our advance. Tomasi was immediately behind me, then Sergeant Makinde Mosi and the rest of the section, followed by the leading platoon of the Ugandans. The going was tricky and hazardous, the track little more than half-a-yard wide, almost as though it had been made not by villagers but by meandering animals, and wound its way confusingly through thick jungle. At any moment we might be caught in an ambush and I was determined that if that happened we would stand and fight to the death, if need be. There must be no running away. The scouts, Private Mawinga and Private Mohammed, were bravely keeping up a good pace, not hanging back as though they were seeing a Japanese behind every tree and bush. As we penetrated deeper and deeper I realised that it would be impossible to get behind the enemy's last reported position without leaving the track which perversely continued east, whereas we needed to go west. With visibility down to less than 10 yards, I was on compass bearings but unless we were extremely careful the entire force might become disorientated so that we, the attackers, could suddenly find ourselves the attacked. I decided to rejoin the main track.

We found the platoon's arms and equipment lying where the troops had cast them as they fled pell-mell. Rifles, webbing harness, groundsheets, haversacks – anything that might slow a man down – littered the track for a good hundred yards. The Japanese had had time to lay boobytraps and in any case we had more important things to do than detach men to retrieve; depending on how events turned out we might be able to do that later. Tense, knowing that we would be in action at any moment, I still had time to feel a deep sense of shame at this evidence of cowardice in the face of the enemy and resolved to write a full report after the battle calling for rigorous disciplinary action against every man-jack.

Mawinga, the leading scout, was already wading thigh-deep across the fast-flowing waters of the chaung when the Japanese opened up with a blasting crash of automatic and rifle fire. I saw him hesitate, half turn, and look back at me. Behind him Mohammed had just entered the water. Five paces back from Mohammed I was still on dry land. 'Charge!' I roared, and as Mawinga and Mohammed threw themselves forward towards the opposite bank I dashed into the water to join them. In a hail of fire from rifles and machine-guns sited to cover the approach to the chaung the three of us, incredibly, crossed unscathed to shelter under the chest-high bank, beneath the noses of the dug-in Japanese. Tomasi had been just too far behind to follow us across the chaung; those five paces and my order to take cover had probably saved his life, I told myself. It was far better that he should be on the 'friendly' bank with the rest of the section under Sergeant Makinde. I needn't worry too much about him now, and could concentrate on our situation.

At the most 5 yards of light vegetation separated us from the enemy. This was real close-quarter stuff. We grinned at one another as I gave the order to throw grenades and pulled the pin out of the first of my four. At my signal each of us lobbed over a grenade and then ducked, waiting for the crashing explosion to follow four seconds later. We knew the Ugandans would be preparing to attack but it must be a little time before they worked out their final plan. Meanwhile, we would try to hang on here for a while. The Japanese were in a real difficulty. They knew how close we were, and I knew we must be causing them casualties, but at present their rifle and machine-gun fire would get us only if we put our heads above the bank. A flank attack along the chaung might be a different story. Bursts of fire cut leaves from the bushes as bullets hummed and whizzed inches above our heads and we tossed over another batch of grenades. Whenever there was a pause in the enemy shooting we popped our heads up and retaliated with Sten and rifle-fire, at the same time wondering how long it would be before the company's attack went in and we could extricate ourselves. I told myself that for all the enemy knew there were now more than just the three of us: our comrades might have crossed the chaung further up and joined us.

Shouts of 'Banzai! Banzai! Banzai!' suddenly rang out, followed by ear-piercing screams. From the racket I estimated that there could be forty or so Japanese – perhaps thirty in their forward position lining the bank and the rest as reserves a little to the rear. More 'Banzais!' and now screams and shouted orders followed at short intervals, doubtless to keep up their morale whilst hoping to lower ours, but Mawinga, Mohammed, and I were far too occupied to worry about Emperor Hirohito living ten thousand years. From the Ugandans there was only a commendable, well-trained silence. A shower of Type 91 grenades – small, black, tumbling objects – now came over in shallow trajectory, seemingly in slow motion, to burst behind us in the water, sending up clouds of spray like miniature depth-charges. This was not a moment to look for small fish floating belly-up. The little battle raged on, broken by sinister pauses suggesting that an assault party could be slithering towards us. To counter this threat we now had to stand upright with our heads above the bank to keep a close look-out, and also to watch the chaung itself in case of a counter-attack approaching from upstream.

I reached for a fresh Sten magazine. The ammunition pouch was empty. Can't be! Mustn't be! But it was – and the explanation was as simple as it was appalling. The two pouches clipped on to my webbing equipment were designed to hold Bren gun magazines, not those for the Sten which were longer so that the pouch-cover stud could not be pressed to secure them. In my headlong dash across the chaung the two magazines in the left-hand pouch must have fallen out and into the water, leaving me with just three magazines, one on the gun and the other two in the right-hand pouch. I had fired off two magazines and all I now had left, I estimated, was about fifteen rounds – half a magazine – instead of seventy-five or so. This was another example of infantrymen fighting with equipment unsuited for its purpose, one which in this case might mean the difference between life and death. My life, my death. I was not pleased.

A slight movement in the vegetation caught the corner of my eye and instinctively I swung round and fired a short burst at it. Sure enough, a Japanese had crawled forward almost to the edge of the bank, as I had feared would happen, and my fire had killed him in the nick of time, before he could drop a grenade on to us. All we could see of his body was his head and shoulders, the rest of him was hidden by a bush. Where there was one enemy soldier there would soon be more, I told myself as another shower of grenades came over, this time falling so close that they burst in flame and smoke on the stones at the water's edge. Mawinga tugged my sleeve. One side of his face was covered in blood streaming from a jagged wound immediately above the corner of his left eye. A half-inch lower and the metal fragment must have pierced his eye-socket. There was no time to take out a First Field Dressing and bandage Mawinga's head; we were fighting for our lives and I decided we could wait only five minutes more for the company's attack to go in. Those minutes took a long time to pass before I ordered Mohammed to guide Mawinga upstream to try to escape across the chaung while I gave covering fire. As the two askaris stole away I lobbed my fourth and last grenade into the yelling, screaming enemy before ducking down again beneath the bank. Another clutch of grenades came over in reply, most of them now well and truly finding my range.

More minutes passed, of silence broken by shooting and screams. I watched with interest as two grenades came over, one of them very low down as though bowled underhand. I knew that this was the one with my name on it and, crouching, instinctively turned to face it as it fell almost at my feet to burst with a brilliant orange flash and a huge, rushing blast. There was a tremendous thump in my right leg. I felt no pain. In a calm, detached way, as though it had happened to somebody else, I noticed that my right trouser leg now had holes in it. By rights I should be dead, for grenades achieve their effects by blast and by the splinters torn from the disintegrating case and this one had fallen so close I could almost have touched it before it exploded. My store of good luck was clearly still not empty, but how much more remained, I wondered? With Mawinga and Mohammed gone and, I hoped, safely away, I knew that unless I extricated myself now it would probably be too late. It was the one thing or the other, I told myself: STAY or GO. I wondered how much longer I would be able to stand, let alone walk. It would have to be GO. I decided I must risk everything with a return crossing of the chaung.

With my last rounds I fired three short bursts into the Japanese to persuade them to keep their heads down, then hurled myself into the water. I was less than halfway across when they spotted me. A hail of bullets zipped and whined past my head, others sending up thin fountains of water beside me as I pushed with all my strength through the thigh-deep water, driving hard to make it to the other side. With every second I expected to go down, shot in the back. Still they missed me, but now I was at the foot of the high bank and must pull myself up out of the water. Surely they couldn't miss such a full-length target? Bullets thudded and thwacked into the bank. With a single mighty heave I was up and over and at once threw myself down into the shallowest of depressions caused by the monsoon rains dripping off the bushes growing parallel to the edge of the chaung. At least I was now on the 'friendly' bank.

I knew that the Japanese could see me, for my slightest movement brought down a storm of humming bullets that ripped through the bushes just an inch or two above me so that some leaves fell on to me and others quivered but did not fall. For some reason that I could not at first fathom the Japanese were unable to finish me off, and then I realised that the God-sent depression had reduced the height of my prone body by a crucial fraction. A heavy silence fell. Who could guess that perhaps as many as two hundred men were concealed in the jungle, manoeuvring to kill one another? The chaung waters gurgled and plashed, and I strained to see whether the Japanese had crossed upstream and were now creeping towards me under the shelter of the bank. With my Sten useless I very slowly, with minimum movement, drew my revolver from its holster. I noticed that my new, shockproof wristwatch had stopped, in all probability knocked out by the grenade's blast. So much for watchmakers' claims!

A leech, black and thin as a bootlace, undulated its way over the toecap of my right boot and made its way unerringly to an eyelet before slithering through to gorge on my blood. I watched with dispassionate interest as it disappeared, reflecting that it could never get out the way it had got in. Renewed bursts of automatic fire broke the silence, followed at once by another storm of exploding grenades so that the jungle echoed and re-echoed to the fury of it all. Were the Japanese about to launch an attack? I was already in no man's land and if they crossed over I would find myself behind them. I eased my panga from its scabbard. That, and my revolver loaded with six rounds, was all I could muster for a last encounter, thanks to equipment unsuited to its purpose.

My right leg was hurting now, sending fierce, jabbing pains

shooting from thigh to foot and back again. It was also beginning to stiffen and I knew that quite soon I might be unable to stand, let alone walk and still less run. God helps those who help themselves. I must take a second big chance. First things first, though. I took from my breast pocket the rexine-framed photograph of my fiancée and had a good look at it before roaring out to the invisible Ugandans, 'I'm pinned down on your side! Give me covering fire!' A moment's silence followed, then the Japanese opened up again with everything they'd got, machine-guns chattering, fusillades of rifle fire, hand grenades going off and yet more screams and shouts of 'Banzai! Banzai! Banzai!' The Ugandans joined in with heavy fire and I jumped to my feet and hurled myself into the jungle to safety, pain forgotten in the relief of finding that I could still move under my own steam. Seconds later I was back among black faces and jungle-green uniforms.

I was greeted by total disbelief, as though I had returned from the dead. The screams that had echoed through the jungle my comrades thought had been mine and the two scouts'. Crossly I told them that those were Japanese screams! A British officer and his brave Tanganyika askaris do not scream! But where was Tomasi? I made my way to the main track in search of the Intelligence Section and spotted them taking cover on the other side. Tomasi saw me, joy and relief written all over his face. Leaping to his feet he started to cross the track towards me. He had taken just five paces when the Japanese machine-gunner covering the approach to the chaung fired a long, long burst.

Tomasi was buried close to the side of the main track, the 'Road to Mandalay' which threads its tortuous way along the floor of the Kabaw Valley. A wooden cross was erected over the grave with his name, rank, and number roughly painted on it:

Pte. Tomasi Liech N40605
36 Bn KAR
Following up the advance, a hygiene reburial squad would

recover his body and take it for interment in a war graves cemetery.

I could not be present when Tomasi was buried by his Intelligence Section comrades in his lonely jungle grave; four askari stretcher-bearers were already carrying me to 60 (East Africa) Field Dressing Station located 3 miles back, slipping and sliding in the deep mud and holding the stretcher above their heads as they waded chest-high across a dozen or more swollen, fast-flowing chaungs. On our way to the rear we halted at an infantry company's bivouac position to give the stretcher-bearers a well-earned rest. Over a mug of that condensed-milk sweet tea which only soldiers know how to brew, my welcoming hosts told me that they had heard our little battle raging and hoped for us. The piercing screams and the shouts of 'Banzai! Banzai! Banzai!' as Mawinga, Mohammed, and I fought from our precarious position on the enemy side of the wide chaung had not carried to their camp, but the clattering bursts of machine-gun fire, the Sten's higher-pitched response, the rifle fire and the boom of Mills bombs and the crack of enemy grenades told their own story. In the hope that the knowledge might come in useful for them, perhaps help to save lives, I explained the Japanese tactics as best I could.

When at last we reached the beginning of drier, firmer ground I was transferred to an open, one-stretcher Jeep ambulance of the American Field Service. The AFS drivers were all young Americans, many of them Quaker conscientious objectors who had volunteered their services in Burma, while others had been rejected as medically unfit for service in the American forces. Throughout the campaign they had proved again and again that no assignment was too dangerous for them and no terrain too difficult in their determination to bring out the wounded from the battle area.

On my return to duty I met the battalion's former medical

Facing page. An improvised jungle operating theatre. John Nunneley under a supply parachute at 60 (East Africa) Field Dressing Station, Kabaw Valley, 1944. Still photograph from an Army Camera Unit cine film.

officer, Captain Paterson. He asked after Tomasi, whom he had come to know well in Abyssinia and Somaliland, and I gave him the sad news. He told me, 'I saw a grave by the trackside and was sure that I recognised the name on the cross'. His words reassured me that Tomasi's body would in due course be recovered and reburied with others of the battalion. Years later, when I requested a photograph of Tomasi's grave, the Commonwealth War Graves Commission wrote in reply, 'Private Thomas Liech has no known grave and is commemorated on Face 103 of the Rangoon War Memorial'. This came as a grievous shock for I knew that the temporary grave's map reference had been properly recorded and reported at the time of burial; and, of course, Captain Paterson had seen the grave some weeks later. What I did not want to believe was the cruel possibility that road building bulldozers and graders might have pushed aside everything in their way – even graves, unknowingly – in the urgency of the British advance, leaving no trace for the follow-up hygiene squads.

Turning Point

WHAT WAS IT made me decide in 1990 that I must meet Louis Allen, author of *Burma: The Longest War*, without delay? His book had been on my shelf all of six years since it was published when I was overcome by a powerful urge to ask him how he came to write this masterly account of the campaign. I tracked him down to the University of Durham, where he taught French literature, discovering also that this gifted man was a theatre and literary critic, television and radio broadcaster, much-in-demand lecturer whose travels took him around the world, and prolific author. During the war he had served with the Intelligence Corps following an eighteen-month course in Japanese at the School for Oriental and African Studies prior to posting to the Burma section of the Combined Services Detailed Interrogation Centre. Within a week we were having lunch together at Durham's County Hotel.

Learning the language inspired Allen to know more of Japan and her people, he told me, and this in turn had driven him throughout the post-war years to encourage and promote reconciliation between Britain and Japan. By chance he discovered that his aim was shared by Ryoichi Sasakawa, a philanthropist who believed that if those who fought one another on the battlefields of Burma could bring themselves to reconciliation, ideally leading to personal and collective friendship, others might follow their example. In 1989 the Great Britain Sasakawa Foundation funded the first visit to Japan by members of the Burma Campaign Fellowship Group, founded by Louis Allen, to meet their former adversaries. We found ourselves getting on so well together that we agreed to continue our discussion at 'Dun Cow Cottage', his residence on the university campus. I found Allen's study a shrine to the printed word, the small room overflowing with books crammed into shelves which lined the walls from floor to ceiling, in teetering piles, and on every flat surface and every chair except his own. Maps, rolled, folded, and hanging, made their own contribution to this scene of comfortable confusion.

'You were in the King's African Rifles', he said, suddenly going off at a tangent. 'Perhaps you can solve a mystery which is baffling a number of us?' With that he handed me a translation from the Japanese headed 'A Personal Memorandum' which had been given to him in Tokyo the previous year. It was written by Sakae Katagiri, who had served in Burma as a captain in 214 Infantry Regiment, 'The White Tigers' of the crack 33 Division which spearheaded the attempted invasion of North-East India in May 1944. Katagiri was a career soldier, now retired, who had risen to the rank of Lieutenant-General in Japan's post-war Self-Defence Forces. The memorandum began: 'For forty-four years since the end of World War II what carries me at times back to old memories is a Royal officer who rushed to death into my position on 22 November 1944. I have spoken about that encounter on various occasions and have long been thinking of an opportunity to convey my feelings about it to his bereaved family. I have decided that on the occasion of a visit to Japan by distinguished members of Royal (i.e. British) veterans to talk about his death in battle in the hope that it might reach the bereaved if I speak further in detail.'

Translated by Tatsuo Kobayashi, Professor Emeritus of Neuro-Psycho Pharmacology at Chiba University, who before the war was medical officer of 64 Sentai, 5 Air Division in China, the memorandum told the story of 'the battle which occurred in the course of the retreat from Imphal by the Imperial Army and which we are calling the battle of Indainggyi that lasted eight days'.

I read on: 'Our 33 Division, after suffering a fatal blow in Imphal, were moving towards the Burma plain by way of Tiddim, Fort White, Kalemyo, and Kalewa. On the way we saw along the narrow path at Kalemyo many sick and injured soldiers lying in swarms. It required at least a week to carry the suffering towards the safer side of the Chindwin River, with trucks whose number could be counted on the fingers of one hand. From the west the Royal (i.e. Indian) 5 Division were pursuing us fiercely with its vanguard reaching Fort White. Around that time, by surprise, the East African 11 Division, which appeared behind the right-hand side of our division, made a dash at Japanese soldiers and drove them out from the Yazagyo area (about 30 kilometres north of Kalemyo) towards the narrow path at Kalemyo. This tactic was apparently taken in order to cut the retreat route and to annihilate our division at Kalemyo. The route from Yazagyo was not paved but the "car road" ran through flat jungle. Along this car road the vanguard of the East African Division charged into and dislodged Japanese platoons and sections one by one by moving round deeply from behind their positions. This tactic was very effective as compared with the one of charging from the front, deploying artillery, and probably was most appropriate to reach the narrow path at Kalemyo in short time.

'Our battalion, which numbered some 500 at the beginning of the Imphal Operation, was reduced to few more than forty through death and wounds. The situation was no different in other battalions in the division. Our position was completely destroyed by delayed-fuse bombs dropped from three Royal aircraft and we had to shift to the north of Kalemyo to stop the advance of the Royal/Indian unit after several vain attempts to build a new position at nearby Fort White. An engineering platoon was allocated to us but, in fact, its number consisted of a sub-lieutenant who was platoon leader, and a non-commissioned officer – and a saw. The forty of us departed Kalemyo in the night and moved north in the direction of Yazagyo along the car road in the jungle, and close to dawn rigged up a position about 10 kilometres north of Kalemyo. I could not believe that the Royal/Indian unit to our front would attack us from behind our position, and that resulted in a sentry missing. The tactic, in fact, was the one commonly used by our army and I resented it greatly – even as far as thinking of killing myself for my unpreparedness. The night fell and fortunately we saw no move by the enemy unit. Then we moved back about 2 kilometres and built a new position once again. This I sited close to the main route and in circle-form to be able to counter-attack any charge from behind. During the following morning reconnoitring soldiers of the Royal/Indian unit were spotted; this was followed by sporadic firing of an 81 mm machine-gun in the afternoon. They seemed to be approaching closer in the rear of our position, as I heard from the sound of covering fire. I could not figure out the numbers of the unit, as there were no human voices heard. That was a well-trained unit. They launched a concentrated firing and I thought they intended to charge into our position the moment the firing stopped. I tried in vain to raise my head to prepare for the attack because the splinters were flying overhead.

'The firing was suddenly halted. I turned my eyes towards the direction from where the firing was heard, and then saw a black soldier running in the opposite direction. I unconsciously shouted, "The enemy is running away!" My men raised their heads and started shooting. To my astonishment, I saw a Royal officer was taking the lead in charging into us with a revolver through a rain of bullets. He finally shot to death a Japanese soldier in the trench but almost instantly he was pierced by the bayonet of the soldier next to the dead soldier. Seeing their officer's death, his men faltered and then withdrew, shouting wildly. I knew the number of attackers was larger than I had thought. Later I found that besides the gallant Royal officer there was a considerable number of dead and wounded on the part of the Royal/Indian unit.

'The East African Division might have judged that a large-scale Japanese position was located here and after that day their artillery attacks lasted more than a week against which we were no more equipped to resist and so further retreated. Incidentally, what I thought was a black soldier running away was that he was trying to untangle a field telephone line, I later found out. In numerous attack and defence battles against the

Royal/Indian unit I could not forget the gallant Royal officer who charged into us with a revolver in a rain of bullets using such adroit tactics. With my deepest respect I wish to dedicate this memorandum to him and his family.'

With absolute certainty I said, 'This does indeed relate to 11 East African Division even though it refers to Indian forces. I know exactly where the action was fought, and when. Katagiri is wrong about the date: it was 3 November not 22 November. I can't say which of two officers killed that day was "the gallant Royal officer" but I will do my best to find out, for the battle was fought against my battalion.' At home I studied the memorandum and compared it with my own journals, records and maps. It was astonishing that this account of one small battle out of thousands of encounters between 14 Army's British, Indian, Gurkha, and East and West African troops and the Japanese 15 Army during almost four years of the campaign should have fallen into my hands, almost certainly the one man most likely to be able to identify the 'gallant Royal officer' so admired by Katagiri and his soldiers.

Allen had brought together a number of former officers who had studied the memorandum without success but concluded that a KAR unit, and not an Indian Army unit, was most likely to have been the one involved. They had impressive Burma qualifications: Tony Jutsum, a fighter-pilot with 60 Squadron, flying first Hurricanes and later Thunderbolts, who gave us bombing and strafing support on 119 sorties in the Kabaw Valley area and now Honorary General Secretary of the Royal Air Force Historical Society; George Shepperson, CBE, Professor Emeritus of Commonwealth and American History at Edinburgh University, was with 13 (Nyasaland) Battalion, KAR; David Shirreff served with the KAR in Abyssinia, Madagascar, where he won a Military Cross, and Burma and subsequently joined the Colonial Administrative Service in East Africa; and Walter Chalmers, Senior Lecturer in Classics and Warden of Sherwood Hall at Nottingham University, who was with the Northern Rhodesia Regiment in Burma. I joined the group and wrote to Sakae Katagiri inviting him to answer questions that might lead to the officer's identity.

In preparing his response he realised that he was in error over the date. 'The mistake', he wrote, 'was caused by my faulty memory and the confusion of battle. Due to this mistake I must apologise that I put you and the other collaborators to much trouble and confusion.' To supplement and illustrate his answers he sent copies of his operational maps – they had been captured from the British and matched my own – and a beautifully-executed, closely-detailed ink-and-watercolour sketch-map of the battlefield, with an explanation of key features translated by Professor Kobayashi. Everything tallied exactly with my knowledge of the area. Parallel with the track, on one side were extensive paddy-field and grass areas giving good visibility to both Japanese and British; on the other side was thick jungle. Tall elephant grass fringed the winding track so that visibility was all too often only a few yards. The absence of other than occasional villages or groups of huts set in the paddy and the presence of others not shown on the map, and the lack of immediately-identifiable features, often combined to make pinpoint accuracy of one's location while on the move difficult to achieve. We studied and identified what Katagiri described as his 'supposed position'.

I was able to confirm from the contours that the upward slope from the track to the Japanese trenches was fairly steep but not so steep as to hinder determined men from charging up it. His other comments and descriptions confirmed my own knowledge. My recollections were vivid because it was my grim duty to recover the bodies of our dead when we occupied the hill feature a week later.

Our next task was to establish the officer's identify. To assist in the search I sought the help of two former 36 KAR officers: Ian Sinclair, a Nairobi banker, and Alastair Mac-Dougall, a Scottish architect, both of whom had been present at the battle. Clues and known facts were checked again and again to ensure that no surviving family members whom we might trace could be caused pain and distress which time might have healed. Three Europeans were killed that day, and many African soldiers. Company Sergeant-Major Jack Widdowes, a Southern Rhodesian, was brought mortally-wounded into the Regimental Aid Post, where he died. We concentrated on Captain Bevan Sellar of the Lancashire Fusiliers, initially reported 'Missing Believed Killed', and Lieutenant Ian Grier, King's Own Scottish Borderers, 'Killed in Action', and moved to the final, vital question. Could Katagiri identify the officer through a sketch of the one and a photograph of the other? MacDougall, a gifted artist, drew a sketch-portrait of Captain Sellar. I recalled that Grier was at school at King William's College in the Isle of Man and that his home was in North-West England. Through school records I traced his brother, Lieutenant-Colonel Burton Grier, and from him obtained a head-and-shoulders portrait photograph.

Notes sent to Katagiri with the two likenesses described Officer 'A' as having dark hair, a dark complexion and a con-spicuous moustache; and Officer 'B' as having fair hair, a light-coloured skin and blue eyes. Badges of rank were not mentioned because this might cause confusion, and in any case, we removed them before going into action. We knew that on this occasion Europeans had not blacked their faces and hands.

Soon I received Katagiri's reply: 'I examined in detail your letters dated July 24, October 6 and December 20 and your request for further information. As the result of this investiga-tion I concluded that the gallant Royal officer who rushed to death into our position on November 3rd was Lieutenant G. I. W. Grier.

'Referring to the evidence of my men I am able to describe his dead body and also to refer to matters on which you wrote to me earlier. He was a tall, middle-weight European young officer with fitted uniform. He was perhaps 180–185 centi-metres in height. He had a revolver in his right hand. He was lying dead with his face turned to the side. He had not blacked his face. He was a white, handsome young European with a peaceful death-mask. We did not verify the colour of his hair

Above Captain Sakae Katagiri, commander, No. 1
Battalion, 214 Infantry Regiment, 'The White Tigers',
recovering from malaria in Maymyo Field Hospital.

Opposite Captain John Nunneley, adjutant, 36 Battalion,
King's African Rifles, recovering from wounds and malaria
in Assam, 1945.

or eyes, nor the badge of his rank. The officer had no map-case or other articles with him, in accordance with battle procedure. He had a light-brown cowboy or boy scout-shape hat (i.e. bush hat). His revolver was especially fine. The length from its muzzle to the bottom was about 20-30 centimetres, and the small butt was made of reddish-brown cherry-tree wood, with ivory carving of a rising dragon. It is my belief that he had always intended to rush bravely to the enemy. His wristwatch was luminous and bore the name "Movado"; or "Mido". I could clearly differentiate between him and the other officer.'

Katagiri's reference to the revolver jogged my memory. I recalled the two of us, Grier and myself, standing among our trenches and discussing our chances of survival – it was soon after dawn 'Stand To' one morning – and each promising to write to the other's girlfriend 'in the event'. It was then that he showed me the revolver he had bought as we passed through Calcutta on our way to the Front. Katagiri was right: it was a fine-looking weapon of .45-inch calibre, with a long barrel and elaborate carving of a dragon on the butt. Grier praised it for its beauty but more especially for its greater stopping-power than the standard Army issue .38-inch Smith & Wesson. With this, the search was over.

The following November I met for the first time Sakae Katagiri and two of his men, Sergeant Ryoichiro Oshima and Corporal Hikozo Kamioka, who fought us in that desperate battle. At the annual reunion in Tokyo of the All-Burma Veterans' Association of Japan I stood on the platform of the Kudan Hall, close to the Yasuakuni Shrine dedicated to all Japanese war dead, and presented Katagiri with an album containing every detail of the search. On behalf of Ian Grier's family and his two regiments I acknowledged Katagiri's 'bushido no nasake' – his warrior's chivalry – which had led at last to the identity of 'the gallant Royal officer'.

★ ★ ★

What had prompted the sudden impulse that led me to Louis Allen? With his death a few short months later Katagiri's memorandum in all probability would have been destroyed or filed away and forgotten. Was it by chance alone that the memorandum had fallen into my hands? And was it no more than coincidence that the date of my meeting with Sakae Katagiri was 3 November 1991, forty-seven years to the day since 'the battle near Indainggyi'?

★ ★ ★

Events that change the course of our lives may steal unsuspected upon us. With the examples of Louis Allen and Sakae Katagiri and Ryoichi Sasakawa before me, I now had reason to place my attitude towards Japan and the Japanese under close scrutiny for the first time since the war.

We who fought the Japanese had at the time little understanding of a military culture which demanded of the soldier, 'When you encounter the enemy regard yourself as an avenger come face to face with your father's murderer. The rigours of the sweltering march may have been but months of watching and waiting for the moment when you may slay this enemy. Here before you is the man whose death will lighten your heart of its burden of brooding anger. If you fail to destroy him utterly, you can never rest in peace. And the first blow is the vital blow.' To us, our almost casual, hate-the-enemy training was impersonal, intended to encourage 'going in with the bayonet' without agonising about it afterwards.

Nor did we understand, at least initially, the carrot-and-stick technique of the Japanese Military Code for Fighting Men which glorified dying for the Emperor, with the promise that the soldier's bones or ashes would be consecrated in the Yasukuni Shrine and the threat that the man who allowed himself to be captured would 'cease to exist' and his disgrace shared by his family. 'Rather than live and bear the shame of imprisonment by the enemy, he should die and avoid leaving behind a dishonourable name.'

Was it any wonder that the Japanese fought with an almost fanatical determination, ready and willing in the last resort to die by their own hand? And in despising their own who surrendered it was surely inevitable that they should despise the enemy soldier who surrendered rather than blow himself up with a grenade held against his chest? The overwhelming mistake that the West made was to expect that fighting Japan would be little different from fighting Germany and Italy.

My sympathy for the suffering endured by those many thousands of troops captured in the Far East and treated with indiscriminate brutality was undiminished and I remained profoundly grateful that I had not had to share their long ordeal. Would I have possessed the moral strength, the nobility of spirit, which distinguished those few former prisoners who brought themselves to forgive, I wondered?

In the final analysis my self-scrutiny decided me that the sustained campaign by Far East prisoner-of-war organisations demanding personal apology by the Emperor of Japan, in words approved in advance by them, coupled with further financial compensation, placed self-interest before national interest; that it had prejudiced public opinion of my own generation against Japan; and, worse, it had passed on hatred and bitterness to two successive, later generations. In the Burma Campaign Fellowship Group I saw the spiritual rewards of reconciliation, and an opportunity to help rebuild a former relationship so that the two countries might go forward as friends and partners, each with a better understanding of the other's culture and way of life, and thinking.

I stood in silent prayer on the flight-deck of a British
Airways 747 thundering through the midnight sky
over Burma as the pilot, Captain Downey, dipped
a wing of the great jet in salute to Tomasi Kitinya,
son of Liech, the brave Luo tribesman
who lies far from the shores of
Lake Victoria.

❧

Weapons of War referred to in the text

GERMAN AIRCRAFT

Messerschmitt Bf109E Fighter
Armament: 2 × 13 mm machine guns
3 × 20 mm cannon
Maximum speed: 387 mph at 38,500 feet ceiling

JAPANESE WEAPONS
Type 38 infantry rifle with 20-inch bayonet
Calibre: 6.5 mm

Bergman (German) sub-machine gun
Rate of fire: 700 rounds per minute
Calibre: 7.63 mm

Type 96 light machine gun with 510 mm rifle bayonet
Rate of fire: 800 rounds per minute
Calibre: 6.5 mm
Purpose: To provide automatic fire for an infantry section
Magazine capacity: 30 rounds

Type 92 medium machine gun
Rate of fire: 450 rounds per minute
Calibre: 7.7 mm

Type 91 hand grenade.
Thrown by hand or fired from grenade launcher
Length: 12.5 cm; diameter: 5 cm
Fuse: 7 to 8 seconds

Type 99 hand grenade.
Fuse: 4 to 5 seconds

Type 89 grenade launcher

Samurai sword
Carried by most officers in battle
Plain leather fist-strap on active service;
decorative cord fist-strap used on parade

Field gun
Calibre: 75 mm

Type 97 tankette
Armament: Type 94 37 mm gun
Maximum speed: 26 mph

'I'- class submarine
Complement: 130
Armament: 8 × 21-inch torpedoes
5.5-inch gun
0.5-inch triple machine gun
Speed: 24 knots
Safe diving depth: 325 feet
Range: 16,000 nautical miles, 24 days at sea

I-27 was one of the most successful Japanese submarines of the war,
sinking twelve ships of 65,995 total tonnage and damaging three of
21,801 total tonnage. I-27 operated off the Australian coast in mid-
1942 and caused havoc on Allied shipping while operating with her
flotilla in the Arabian Gulf in 1943. I-27 was the fifty-third Japanese
submarine sunk. I-class submarines carried the two-man midget
submarines that attacked Pearl Harbour and Sydney, Durban, and
Diego Suarez harbours.

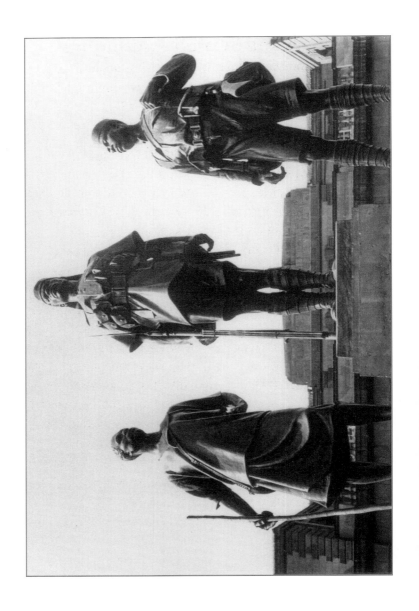

English and Swahili inscriptions

on the Dar es Salaam Askari Monument
built in memory of the African troops who fought
in the Great War of 1914–18

THIS
IS TO THE MEMORY OF
THE NATIVE AFRICAN
TROOPS WHO FOUGHT:
TO THE CARRIERS WHO
WERE THE FEET AND
HANDS OF THE ARMY:
AND TO ALL OTHER MEN
WHO SERVED AND DIED
FOR THEIR
KING AND COUNTRY
IN EASTERN AFRICA
IN THE GREAT WAR
1914
1918

IF YOU FIGHT FOR
YOUR COUNTRY
EVEN IF YOU DIE
YOUR SONS
WILL REMEMBER
YOUR NAME

HUU NI UKUMBUSHO
WA ASKARI WENYEJI
WA AFRIKA WALIOPIGANA
KATIKA VITA KUU NA NI
UKUMBUSHO PI A
WA WAPAGAZI AMBAO
WALIKUWA MIGUU NA
MIKONO YA MAJESHI. NI
UKUMBUSHO PIA WA WATU
WOTE WALIOTUMIKA WAAKAFA
KWA AJILI YA MFALME
NA NCHI YAO, KATIKA AFRIKA
MASHARIKI KWENYI VITA
KUU TOKA MWAKA 1914
MPAKA 1918. UKIPIGAMIA
NCHI YAKO NJAPO
UMEKUFA WATOTO WAKO
WATALIKUMBUKA JINA LAKO.

Glossary

askari soldier or policeman (Arabic and Swahili)
assegai spear, weapon of the Zulu armies
baraza council-house; meeting; gathering (Swahili)
bibi woman (Swahili)
bimbashi lowest British commissioned rank in Sudan Defence
  Force; originally equivalent to colonel in the Egyptian Army.
  (Turkish)
bush uncultivated land, forest, 'the beyond'
bwana master. 'Bwana mkubwa' – big master (Swahili)
chagoul canvas or leather water bag. (EA: Anglo-Indian)
choo pron. 'cho'; latrine (Swahili)
chop-box European's safari 'tuck box' of delicacies
debe 4-gallon petrol/oil can (derived from iron coffee measure)
  serving many functions
duka shop or store, usually run by Indian trader
effendi lord, term of respect (Sudan; EA); civilian designation
  approximate to 'Mr' (Turkish)
feranji foreigner
jambo greetings (Swahili)
kharif seasonal westerly wind, Somalia
Khedive Viceroy of Egypt under Ottoman Empire (e.g. 'The
  Khedive Ismail')
kiboko rawhide whip (EA; KAR), usually made from rhinoceros or
  hippopotamus hide
kipande a piece; bundle of employers' references. Also **kitabu**
  book (Swahili)
mfecane a crushing
mganga witch-doctor
moto fire, heat, hot (Swahili)
mpishi a cook (Swahili)
mtoto small boy; kitchen assistant (Swahili)
mzungu white man. pl. wazungu (Swahili)

ngoma tribal dance, lit. drum (Swahili)
ngonjwa ya bibi venereal disease (Swahili)
nullah dried up watercourse
panga bush knife; machete (Swahili)
pombe beer (Swahili)
posho rations, i.e. millet porridge (Swahili)
safari journey (EA)
safi clean, 'pure', e.g., 'speaks safi Swahili'
sana adj. very, as in 'moto sana' – 'very hot'
shauri consult, advice, affair, matter (Swahili)
shauri ya mungu lit. 'God's affair'
shifta marauding bandits, esp. Northern Frontier District, Kenya; Ethiopia; Somalia
sundowner drink taken at 6 p.m. (and thereafter)
Swahili East African lingua franca developed for trading purposes, supposedly from the Arabic 'Suahele' – 'man of the coast'.
   'Ki (kitchen)-Swahili' and 'Ki-settler' – ungrammatical Swahili as spoken by settlers
valise bedding roll

Note
Swahili is a Bantu language which over time has adopted and absorbed words from diverse sources, so 'Bantu-ising' them that speakers do not recognise them as 'foreign' words. Most of these words have been introduced into Swahili by Arab and Indian traders; some by German and Portuguese colonists; and many by the British. – D.V. Perrott, Preface to *Concise Swahili and English Dictionary*, published by Hodder & Stoughton.

Bibliography

ALLEN, Charles (ed.). *Tales from the Dark Continent* (London: Andre Deutsch & The British Broadcasting Corporation, 1979; Macdonald Futura, 1981)

ALLEN, Louis. *Burma: The Longest War* (London: Dent, 1984)

BULL, Bartle. *Safari: A Chronicle of Adventure* (New York: Viking, 1988)

EVANS, Geoffrey and Anthony BRETT JAMES. *Imphal* (London: Macmillan, 1962)

FARSON, Negley. *Last Chance in Africa* (London: Gollancz, 1949)

FEATHERSTONE, Donald. *Victorian Colonial Warfare: Africa* (London: Blandford, 1992)
Captain Carey's Blunder (London: Blandford, 1990)

FOX, James. *White Mischief* (London: Jonathan Cape, 1992)

HALL, Richard. *Stanley: An Adventurer Explored* (London: Collins, 1974)

HANLEY, Gerald. *Monsoon Victory* (London: Collins, 1946)
Warriors and Strangers (London: Hamish Hamilton, 1971)

HUXLEY, Elspeth. *The Flame Trees of Thika* (London: Chatto & Windus, 1959; Penguin Books, 1962)

JEAL, Tim. *Livingstone* (London: Heinemann, 1973)

JULY, Robert W. *A History of the African People* (New York: Faber & Faber)

KIRBY, S. Woodburn. *History of the Second World War*, vol. iv *The War against Japan* (London: HMSO, 1965)

KNIGHT, Ian. *Zulu: Isandhlwana and Rorke's Drift* (London: Windrow & Greene, 1992)

LABAND, John (ed.). *Lord Chelmsford's Zululand Campaign 1878–1879* (London: Army Records Society and Alan Sutton Publishing, 1994)

MASON, Philip. *A Matter of Honour* (London: Jonathan Cape, 1974)

MEINERTZHAGEN, Richard. *Kenya Diary* (London: Oliver & Boyd, 1957; Eland Books paperback, 1983)

MILLER, Charles. *The Lunatic Express* (New York: Ballantine, 1971)

MOOREHEAD, Alan. *The White Nile* (London: Hamish Hamilton, 1960)

MORRIS, Donald. *The Washing of the Spears: The Rise and Fall of the Zulu Nation* (London: Jonathan Cape, 1966)

MOYSE-BARTLETT, Hubert. *The King's African Rifles. A Study of the Military History of East and Central Africa, 1890-1945* (Aldershot: Gale & Polden, 1956)

NUNNELEY, John (ed.). *Tales from the Burma Campaign 1942–1945* (London: Burma Campaign Fellowship Group, 1998)

PACHAI, Bridglal (ed.). *Livingstone: Man of Africa. Memorial Lectures, 1873-1973* (London: Longman, 1971)

PAKENHAM, Thomas. *The Scramble for Africa* (London: George Weidenfeld & Nicolson, 1991)

STISTED, Georgiana. *The True Life of Captain Sir Richard Burton.* (London: Ward, Lock reprints, 1970)

TRZEBINSKI, Errol. *The Kenya Pioneers* (London: Heinemann, 1985)

WARNER, Peggy and SENO, Sadao. *The Coffin Boats: Japanese Midget Submarine Operations in the Second World War* (Leo Cooper in association with Secker and Warburg, 1986)

WYKES, Alan. *Snake Man: The Story of C. J. P. Ionides* (London: Alan Sutton Publishing, 1984)